THEORY H.O.W.

How Organizations Could Work

THEORY H.O.W.
How Organizations Could Work

Harold E. Cavallaro

Carol A. Ptak

Specialty Publishing Company

Library of Congress Cataloging-in-Publication.

Printed in the United States of America
First Edition

10 – digit ISBN 0-9755199-3-X
13 – digit ISBN 978-0-9755199-3-6

1. Operations 2. Management 3. Continuous Improvement
I. Title.
10 9 8 7 6 5 4 3 2 1

Theory H.O.W.
    How Organizations Could Work
Harold E. Cavallaro   Carol A. Ptak
176 p.: ill
Bibliographical references and index

Specialty Publishing Company, Inc.
135 E. St. Charles Rd., Carol Stream, Il 60188
www.specialtypub.com

Specialty Publishing books are available at special quantity discounts to use as premiums or for corporate educational training programs. For more information, please contact Special Books Manager at 630-933-0844.

Table of Contents

Acknowledgements

As you navigate your way through life there are those that influence your direction and support you along the way. Clearly without this guidance and input the journey would be much longer and certainly much more difficult. And such a journey it has been—life on the road is bittersweet and has had as much an impact on me personally as those who share my life. My parents always told me—'You can do anything you put your mind to.'—and I must have listened somewhere along the way. So thanks to them for first setting me on the right path.

My wonderful wife Nasrin has been a great co-pilot all these years and has mostly played the role of single mom while I travel from client-to-client every week. Without her love, support, understanding, and extreme patience I could not have accomplished so much.

I have had the opportunity to work alongside some of the best professionals in the industry. Their brotherhood, coaching, and sharing of ideas has enabled me to grow both professionally and personally. We all shared in the development and application of new improvement techniques as well as the challenges presented at each new client opportunity. M.L. Srikanth and I cut our teeth together back in 1978 and began this wonderful journey when we first met Dr. Eli Goldratt. Mike Maturo has also been one of those friends for over 25 years and has contributed greatly throughout the years. In addition I would also like to thank both Scott Robertson for his partnership and Jack Sheehan for his continued involvement and support. At the risk leaving anyone else out by trying to list you all—I would rather just say thanks for the camaraderie.

Good teachers come along once in a great while, great teachers are rare. I want to thank Dr. Eli Goldratt for giving me the chance to join his team back in 1978–1979 as number four of the original U.S. TOC gang—thanks for teaching me to really 'think' and to look at the world from a completely different perspective. You made me a promise when we first met—join me and see the world, and you added with a chuckle, you may never see your friends and family again! You actually kept both those promises.

It goes without saying, that all of the work presented in this text would have no validity or context without the invaluable input directly or indirectly though all the years of working with the many manufacturing organizations around the world where I had the privilege of participating in their organizations' improvement efforts. They are too numerous to mention but my thanks goes out to all.

Doug Whelan—client, student, friend, and coach—a special thanks for being all of these and more. I have benefited greatly from your friendship and guidance both on the shop floor and in our personal and family lives.

Theory H.O.W., How Organizations Could Work would still be a collection of notes and ideas without the support of our publisher and friend, Peggy Smedley. In addition, Marco Carating's creative and artistic talent helped us create all of the great illustrations for both the textbook and workbook. A special thanks to both of you.

And finally, New Haven, Conn., and Seattle, Wash., are three thousand miles apart. Some days that seemed like an enormous distance—and yet with our crazy lives and schedules we were able to overcome the challenge and successfully collect our ideas to create this work. Carol Ptak is an outside the box thinker, a visionary, the consummate professional, and a great cook! It's been a pleasure to share this podium—thanks partner.

Harold Cavallaro

Acknowledgements—Carol Ptak

Theory H.O.W. was no more than some scratching on a napkin as Harold and I discussed the title over a drink at an airport (where else?) after a conference where we had both presented. This crazy idea continued to develop over the next couple of years of doing something very different for the manufacturing company that is assaulted daily by the hoard of three letter acronyms. The process was at times slow but at times exhilarating as together we uncovered some big "ah-ha" that neither would have seen alone. My greatest appreciation goes to Dr. Eli Goldratt for his insight that put the final key in the lock to breakthrough that final block wall to make this book a reality. Eli, you are always ahead of your time and I am so grateful for what you have taught me as we worked together on *Necessary but not Sufficient* and what you have developed since then. To me, listening to your presentation in Barcelona was finding the cipher to an unbreakable code of jumbled ideas scrambling around in my brain. Without you this book would still be in process.

Echoing Harold's comments, I cannot thank Peggy Smedley enough for her continued dedication to American Manufacturing, her belief in this book, and her patience as we worked through the process. Peggy, you are a rare friend indeed. I am so grateful you came into my life.

Many friends supported, encouraged, and aided the writing of this book. One person in particular continues to be my best friend, inspiration, and source of strength. Over 27 years ago we made the promise to share good times and bad, richer and poorer, sickness and health. Little did we know what adventures those promises would bring! Looking back, we have been there and done that, and bought the T-shirt—and the ranch. Your quiet strong faith always helped pull me through those really hard times and continues to inspire me to become a better person. Your great sense of humor made the bad times seem more like the good times. This book is dedicated to my very best friend and husband, Jim.

Carol Ptak

Preface

Theory H.O.W., How Organizations Could Work was written to enable small and medium-size manufacturing companies to isolate the vital few actions necessary to transform the company to achieve its desired goal. This book will help you identify the critical cause and effect relationships that are affecting the business and preventing it from achieving this goal. With the Theory H.O.W. approach, you will be able to formulate strategies that are supported by specific tactical actions, systems, technology, and other tools to achieve your desired sustainable competitive advantage. Some of the material at the beginning of the book may look familiar and not be breakthrough thought to you. However, these building blocks are carefully selected to begin to build the foundation used later in the book. Don't be fooled by this familiarity, there are specific reasons why each topic was included. Like the keystone in an archway, it can be the smallest thing that holds everything else together.

In order to compete in today's global economy and to gain significant strategic advantage, manufacturing companies are striving to become part of the extended enterprise. This requires them to redefine their position in the total supply chain—from raw materials all the way through to the final customer. Looking forward, manufacturers will continue to face more challenges than ever. World economic constraints such as labor and material costs, pressure from both suppliers and upstream manufacturers and faster deliveries through complex distribution channels increasingly challenge the manufacturer's existence.

World-class manufacturers lead in their industries because they've learned to successfully navigate even the most treacherous business challenges to constantly deliver results and performance that puts them at the top of their specific industry group. Successful companies and organizations measure themselves on both financial and operational metrics—and focus on what they do best. It requires them to constantly reassess this position while simultaneously improving the process, eliminating waste, increasing throughput, accelerating flow, reducing cost, and then leveraging these improvements with innovative supply chain solutions and technology.

What operational improvements does your business need to make? Where do you want your business to be in three years? Five years? Or even just this financial year? How are you going to get there?

Theory H.O.W., How Organizations Could Work, is focused on answering those questions. Working through this process and adopting this methodology can help you develop your specific improvement roadmap. It can help you to better understand your business from all angles and help your organization in aligning your Strategy, Processes, Technology, and People to realize the full potential of your assets and resources. This is a combination of the right attitude and the right know how that can assist you in streamlining the business, eliminating waste, and empowering your people.

For centuries, great chefs from around the world have worked and reworked some of the same recipes. Each experienced culinary professional makes the slightest adjustments to the ingredients or the process in order to improve the essence or enhance the flavor. This is required to meet their client's greater expectations and demands and to keep pace with the ever changing and fast paced world. Consultants and business professionals, like the great chefs, are continuously refining their skills, reworking their 'recipes' for success, and looking for new tools to introduce into the process on the journey to manufacturing perfection. Even though the manufacturing world and the supply chain have continued to change and expand rapidly over the past few years the basic building blocks that are the very foundation of this discipline have and will always remain the same.

The scientific world thrives on researching and understanding the true causes and effects of physical nature. The basic building block is their ability to define everything with elements and characteristics. Similarly, the consulting world has relied on defining everything and anything. Many hours of research have been done in studying organizational behavior and their ability to be effective and productive.

The backbone behind the Theory H.O.W. approach is really a combination of these key elements—the ability to classify, define, or characterize key business elements, and their effects on business performance and the organization's ability to produce greater results by having a much clearer understanding of how to get the job done.

This book has been specifically designed for manufacturing organizations that want to aggressively challenge the status quo. It is not a textbook, but a workbook and process map that you and your team can follow. When you have completed the diagnostic process you won't have just a list of improvement activities. You will have assembled an extremely detailed profile of the entire business. This profile, which is simply defined by both Static Enterprise Characteristics and Dynamic Enterprise Characteristics, is the basis for building and executing the improvement program again and again. Most importantly is your knowledge of what to do first that will bring the highest level of return on investment.

This book and the Theory H.O.W. approach will bring your team through five phases. This starts with material that may be very familiar to you. However, by the time you reach the Diagnostic phase you can expect to be in unfamiliar territory. The improvement phase will bring new clarity to this unfamiliar territory.

▶ The Preparation Phase includes establishing your team infrastructure and other basic necessities required for any successful endeavor like this. This consists of how to choose team members and coaches, and what education and training will be required.

▶ The Learning Phase incorporates detail about the Theory H.O.W. approach and begins the process of establishing an initial company profile. This phase will lead your company through the development of your organization's static enterprise characteristics. In this section you will also develop the correct set of measures to support this profile.

▶ The Diagnostic Phase includes the dynamic elements of the Theory H.O.W. approach. This phase builds on the profile established in the learning phase to identify a possible improvement path.

▶ The Improvement Phase will lead your team through the interpretation of your static and dynamic analysis. This phase begins the construction of an optimal improvement plan.

▶ The Implementation Phase will describe how the plan determined in the improvement phase can be implemented in your company.

How to use this book

In order to get the best results from this book and the process— you have to really use and abuse this book and its accompanying workbook, *Theory H.O.W. To.*

Even if you are used to protecting your books from the slightest pencil mark—forget about it, as you will need to interact with the book, save ideas, share your findings with other team members, and get their ideas.

This book presents the elements of developing a transformation process in a practical and pragmatic way.

Both *Theory H.O.W.* and *Theory H.O.W. To* are written in a format that is easy to read and easy to follow. The Theory H.O.W. approach, self-assessment tools, and diagnostics provide the team with what is necessary to guide them through the process.

The H.O.W. Audience

This book has been written to be used by executives, team leaders, champions and improvement team members and is dedicated specifically to the manufacturing industry. It is meant to be used by cross functional teams led by an executive to initiate the transformation process or to reenergize an existing team to take the next leap of innovation and breakthrough improvement.

The Theory H.O.W. Approach

The Theory H.O.W. approach is fully described in this text. In order to support the changes necessary in an organization, we have also prepared an accompanying workbook, *Theory H.O.W. To*. This contains more detail on the diagnostics and transformation process including the necessary forms and checklists.

Using a Journal

Life is a journey of learning. So is transformation and continuous improvement. As you travel through this new approach you are going to encounter new ideas, identify both new opportunities and roadblocks, have questions, and revel in your own intuitiveness. Don't waste a minute or a thought—write it down!

If every team member does the same, you can use that information as you work through the program together.

To carry the process even further, consider keeping a Team Journal to accumulate the team's ideas, thoughts, and actions. With the great results you will achieve, others will want to know how you did it. Be ready to share the story!

Reference Information

Theory H.O.W. To is available as a workbook to make the process easier for the team and to ensure that you don't miss a critical step.

As you read this book you may encounter new terms that you may not have seen before. They are used in a very specific way. There is a Glossary of Terms in the Appendix of the workbook for you to refer to as you go through the process.

Summary

Different businesses can benefit in different ways. But when manufacturers can identify, excel, and exploit key operational areas, they strengthen their core competencies—and outpace their competition. We would love to hear from you as you work through this process.

Harold Cavallaro
Carol Ptak

Foreword

You may have picked up this book because you know that you have a manufacturing problem and you realize what you are currently doing no longer works. You suspect that without some radical change your business might fail. Or you may have picked it up because you are wondering what all the talk of business improvement is about. Either way, if you are in manufacturing you cannot afford to relax and feel that everything will be all right once the storm blows over.

Competition somewhere in the world has begun to hurt your business in a noticeable way, or it soon will.

No matter what state your business is in, you can always take another hard look at where you are and improve the company's bottomline. Unless you are currently upstaging your competitors in every facet of your business, you need to be improving your business practices, so that you will stay in the forefront in your industry.

Every doctor that you might visit will at least check your blood pressure, pulse rate, temperature and respiration. Similarly, every business should routinely measure throughput, investment, operating expense, cycle time, and delivery performance. Too many companies fail to have a consistent set of measurements and flounder because they do not understand if they are making progress. In your business, if these measures are not improving year after year, you can be assured that the patient is in decline compared to its worldwide competition.

Knowing that your business needs to improve and knowing how to do it are two different things. *Theory H.O.W., How Organizations Could Work* provides a comprehensive way to look at your business to find and fix the vital few things that will make all of your measures improve. Improving these key measurements leads inevitably to improving profitability, which is the goal of all businesses. The textbook in combination with the *Theory H.O.W. To* workbook is a powerful combination that will withstand the test of time.

Carol Ptak and Harold Cavallaro are internationally known experts in the fields of process improvement, measurement systems, and manufacturing control. Carol and Harold have combined years of practical experience in hundreds of manufacturing operations in developing their approach. I have experienced their approach firsthand with outstanding results in multiple instances and so I commend their book to your reading. Their advice can make a signficant difference in your business.

J. Douglas Whelan
Former President & COO, Board Member
Wyman-Gordon Company

Chapter 1
What Is
Theory H.O.W.?

Introduction

Theory H.O.W., How Organizations Could Work will help any size organization, but was especially written to enable small to medium manufacturing companies to isolate the vital few actions necessary to transform the company to achieve its desired goal. This chapter begins the process that will help a company identify the critical cause and effect relationships that are affecting the business and preventing it from achieving this goal.

Theory H.O.W. is a pragmatic "HOW TO" approach that can provide manufacturing executives with a comprehensive view of their world and the means to drive transformation and significant business improvements. *Theory H.O.W.* delivers:

- ▶ A repeatable process.

- ▶ An optimal starting point diagnosis for you and your team.

- ▶ A comprehensive methodology for developing effective solutions.

- ▶ The development and motivation plan for the improvement champions and teams.

- ▸ An implementation plan to accelerate incremental and breakthrough improvement.

- ▸ A way of evaluating results and changing the process to affect improvement in process effectiveness.

- ▸ Guidelines and recommendations to execute that plan—a move to action.

By this alignment and activation of the company's people, processes, and technology, an on-going, sustainable competitive advantage can be achieved. You may be saying, "Words we've heard before!"

Of course! So why is this book and its approach different than any other?

Many hours of research, observation, and evaluation have been spent in assessing how organizations behave and why transformation to achieve a desired goal is so difficult. Based on this research, different theories on behavior and effectiveness have been developed. These theories have evolved over time and some have kept pace with our ever changing world. They are worth reviewing here as background for *Theory H.O.W.* as we believe that in keeping with the times—this is the next logical progression.

Theory X

Theory X assumes that the average worker is inherently lazy and requires supervision. Theory X further assumes that:

- ▸ The average worker dislikes work and avoids work whenever possible.

- ▸ To induce adequate effort, the supervisor must threaten punishment and exercise careful supervision.

- ▸ The average worker avoids increased responsibility and seeks to be directed.

The manager that accepts Theory X normally exercises authoritarian-type control over workers and allows little participation during decision making. Theory X employees generally favor lack of responsibility, especially in decision making. Theory X has been shown over time to be an ineffective way to run a business. However, certain times in the organization's development still require a Theory X approach. For example, when a company must go through a disruptive change in order to survive, a Theory X approach used by a strong leader can be very effective to set the strategy.

Theory Y

According to Theory Y, employees are willing to get the job done without constant supervision. Theory Y further assumes that:

▶ The average worker wants to be active and finds the physical and mental effort on the job satisfying.

▶ Greatest results come from willing participation, which will tend to produce self-direction toward goals without coercion and control.

▶ The average worker seeks opportunity for personal improvement and self-respect.

The manager who accepts Theory Y normally advocates participation and a management-employee relationship. However, in working with professionals, especially engineers, special care must be exercised because these individuals often pride themselves on their ability to find a better way (from their perspective) to achieve the end result regardless of the cost. As these folks continue to search for the "best" answer they will continue as long as their executives will allow since accepting "good enough" is never considered.

As Theory Y came into more common practice, there can be a tendency for executives to abdicate their leadership role, leaving the organization to determine strategy through collaboration. In the current hyper competitive market, the response time to develop strategy by committee is insufficient to maintain a competitive advantage. This is where the Theory X approach can be superior. Attempting to develop strategy by committee tends to look like an amalgamation of personal agendas rather than a real strategy with a desired goal.

Theory Z

According to Ouchi's Theory Z, workers want to build cooperative and close working relationships with those they work with as well as the people who work for them. Theory Z further assumes that;

▶ Workers have a high need to be supported by the company in a family type arrangement.

▶ The focus is on having a strong company philosophy and this becomes a important social institution.

▶ Decisions are made by consensus with a strong sense of order and dedication to the job from each employee.

▶ Long-range staff development focuses on becoming generalists rather than specialists.

Theory Z is a highly participative approach and demands that managers have a high level of trust in the employees. The goal is to have long term relationships with employees where they continue to grow and develop in their skills and knowledge. Similar to Theory Y, an exclusive focus on Theory Z puts a company at a disadvantage when substantial changes need to be made quickly.

Theory H.O.W.

Theory H.O.W. brings the clear vision and direction from Theory X, the willing participative management style of Theory Y, and the culture driven effectiveness of Theory Z to set the organization on the right path for success. In addition, the Theory H.O.W. approach also incorporates the specific tactical actions, systems, technology, and other tools to help you to achieve your desired sustainable competitive advantage.

Embedded in *Theory H.O.W.* are the beliefs that the people in the company:

- ▶ Want to improve the performance or effectiveness of the specific manufacturing operation or process they work on or manage.
- ▶ Care deeply about the overall quality of their work.
- ▶ Want to have pride in the finished product or service provided by the company.
- ▶ Spend a significant amount of their time correcting mistakes previously made at their work station or by someone else.
- ▶ Are afforded very little time to assist in the improvement process or outcome.
- ▶ Are tired of hearing the litany of conflicting desires from the management team.
- ▶ Would love to be able to make the motivational speeches and conference calls just go away.

The Theory H.O.W. Approach

The Theory H.O.W. approach contains three basic zones and the linkages between those zones.

The three basic zones are Vision, Business Rules, and Technology. While a company can technically begin anywhere on the Theory H.O.W. cycle, the best results are achieved when starting with the vision. The Theory

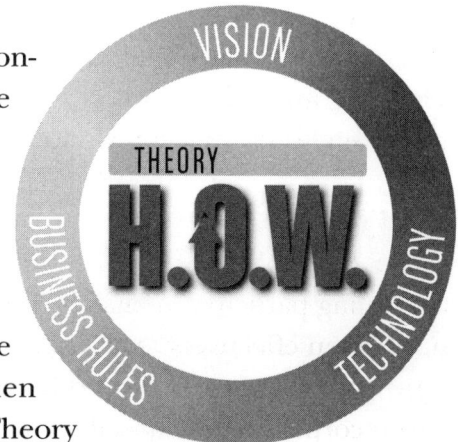

H.O.W. approach combines several well-known operation improvement methodologies with a diagnostic model to establish a next steps plan for the enterprise. However, unlike any of these methodologies or approaches, *Theory H.O.W.* recognizes that every company is unique.

In the research for this book, the major discovery was that a company derives its competitive advantage from that uniqueness. The traditional process improvement or industry best practice approaches attempt to make companies look more like each other or fit companies into a standardized approach. Industry analysts simplify complex issues into a 2x2 matrix with a presumption that every company desires the same end result—the upper right hand quadrant. This is a great disservice to the manufacturing company.

There are things that are given within the business environment and within the company. Think of companies as being like different animals—an elephant may want to run like a cheetah, but its physical size just will not allow it. Similarly the cheetah may desire the size and strength of an elephant, but it is just not built that way. Each kind of animal has different potential and a different way to compete for food.

In *Theory H.O.W.* these are called SEC (static enterprise characteristics). This is not to say that an elephant can't be faster or a cheetah larger. These are dynamic characteristics that can be defined once there is an understanding of what you are. In *Theory H.O.W.* this action plan depends on the items that can be changed inside a company or what is called DEC (dynamic enterprise characteristics).

The Theory H.O.W. approach helps you define your goal, understand what and where you are, and then how to isolate the vital few actions necessary to transform your company to achieve its desired goal.

The Preparation Phase

The preparation phase includes establishing your business team infrastructure and other basic necessities required for any successful endeavor like this. This consists of how to choose team members and coaches, and what education and training will be required.

Not every project will require every role on the team described in the section on the preparation phase. However, considering up front what resources are really needed can help get the project started on the right track.

The Learning Phase

The learning phase provides the detail of the Theory H.O.W. model in context with the static enterprise characteristics for your company. Chapter 4, The Theory H.O.W. Approach begins this process with a description of each of the Theory H.O.W. zones and the interaction between those zones in more detail. The static enterprise characteristics are defined in Chapter 5, Static Enterprise Characteristics. You will also be guided through the process of developing the correct set of measures to expand your profile. Once these have been completed then you are ready to move to the diagnostic phase.

The Diagnostic Phase

The diagnostic phase described in Chapter 6, Dynamic Enterprise Characteristics, pulls the appropriate information from the profile completed in Chapter 4, The Theory H.O.W. Approach and Chapter 5, Static Enterprise Characteristics and begins to the process of gleaning the vital few focus items from amidst the many useful items identified.

The diagnostic stage is where you will understand and complete the dynamic enterprise characteristic profile. From this data a diagnosis can be made about the next logical move for the company. Once that has been completed then the company can evaluate its next move based on the dynamic enterprise characteristics once again. The Theory H.O.W. approach has been developed to provide a repeatable ongoing improvement process for any type of company.

The Improvement Phase

The best diagnosis is meaningless unless the company does something with it. The improvement phase as described in Chapter 7, Defining an Improvement Solution, identifies specific solution alternatives and helps choose the most appropriate solution to put into action. In the improvement phase the implementation and contingency plans are developed to help ensure the plans' overall success.

The Implementation Phase

Implementation is where all the investigation and planning work that has been done becomes a reality. The implementation phase as described in Chapter 8 brings the company to achieving its desired transformation. The best ideas without implementation are a waste of the time and talents of the people who developed them. Even a bad idea well executed is better than a great idea sitting in a book on the shelf. Based on this first implementation step, the stage is set for the next step and the next in a never ending journey.

Figure 1.1 **The *Theory H.O.W.* Content Map**

THE PREPARATION PHASE	THE LEARNING PHASE	THE DIAGNOSTIC PHASE	THE IMPROVEMENT PHASE	THE IMPLEMENTATION PHASE

• What Is Theory H.O.W.
• The Theory H.O.W. Approach
• Why Theory H.O.W.
  - The Challenge
  - The Constraints
• Getting Ready for Theory H.O.W.
	• The Holistic Approach
	• Learning the Background Techniques
	• How to Develop the Initial Plan
	• Static Enterprise Characteristic Evaluation
	• Develop Your Internal and External Supply Chain Profile
	• Develop Your Internal and External Product Flow Diagrams
	• Develop Your Inventory Profile
	• Develop Your Company Performance Profile
		• Dynamic Enterprise Characteristics Analysis
		• Market Performance Evaluation
		• Evaluate Your Constraints
		• Evaluate Your Company Challenges and Opportunities
			• How to Create the Improvement Plan—Current Reality to Future Reality Based on Analysis	• How to Prepare the Improvement Plan
				• How to Market and Sell the Plan
				• Book Summary

Chapters 1–3	Chapters 4–5	Chapter 6	Chapter 7	Chapters 8–9

Summary

This chapter begins your journey with *Theory H.O.W.* as your guide. This book has been developed through a lifetime of research, observation, and experience. Think of the book you are holding as a cookbook, teaching you about ingredients and meal preparation and helping you understand what meal goes with what situation. The *Theory H.O.W. To* workbook provides the specific recipes and examples of successful meals that have been served with this methodology. It is our hope that you will use both these volumes often to achieve a sustainable competitive advantage for your company.

References
Theory Z, Ouchi

Chapter 2
Understanding the Problem "Why H.O.W. Now?"

Introduction

The world of manufacturing has changed. The unifying goal to make money now and into the future has not changed from 1984 when Dr. Eli Goldratt wrote *The Goal*. However, the world in which the manufacturing company must compete has changed dramatically. By all expert assessments this rate of change will continue to do so for the foreseeable future. Executives and other managers are discovering that the traditional common practice approaches taught and trusted for so many years no longer work. These executives are inundated with a never ending assault of new ideas. They struggle to separate the wheat from the chaff to determine which can really contribute to their success. The clock speed of the manufacturing business world is increasing at rapid pace. There is no time to make a mistake.

The Manufacturing Challenge

Now, more than ever, we need to rethink the nature of management—not only in manufacturing, but in all industries. Most visibly in manufacturing, U.S. employment in manufacturing peaked at 19 million in 1979 and has been on a downward trend since.

Many people fear this is due to outsourcing and offshoring to countries like China and the Far East. However, the real situation is even more daunting. Between 1995 and 2002, more than 31 million factory jobs disappeared from the top 20 global economies. During those same years global productivity increased by 30%. At the same time American productivity saw a 20% increase.

Incidentally, this pattern is not unique. This has been seen before in the agriculture industry. In 1810 the population in the U.S. was 11 million with 85% of people in agriculture—it took 9 million people to feed 11 million. By 2001 only 4.8 million U.S. agricultural workers fed 290 million people and provided substantial exports. In addition to the general rise in manufacturing productivity, significant manufacturing capacity has been added in China, Korea, Malaysia, Thailand, Vietnam, and the eastern European countries. Not surprisingly the world of scarce capacity in the mid 1990s has been turned upside down. Now all types of manufacturing capacity is plentiful around the world.

Manufacturing and Technology Evolution

The technological world has also evolved dramatically in the last five decades. A symbiotic relationship exists between increasing computing power and the development of new technological tools. Rudimentary MRP (material requirements planning) systems emerged in the 1950s. This technique evolved as computer systems increased in power to include capacity planning, called 'closed loop MRP.' When financial capabilities were integrated in the 1980s, the next evolution was comprehensive MRP II (manufacturing resource planning) systems. Computers continued to increase in power. Then it was possible to manage and track all the resources across an enterprise using ERP (enterprise resource planning) systems. By the mid 1990s, in recognition of demand exceeding supply, the software industry recognized that there was scarce capacity. If this scarce capacity could be kept working on the most profitable parts, the manufacturing enterprise should realize dramatic bottomline results. Sophisticated

APS (advanced planning, and scheduling) systems were then developed that optimized the production schedule to maximize the capacity utilization. At the core of this evolution is the use of computers to manage inventory.

Figure 2.1 **Technological evolution in manufacturing— conventional wisdom**

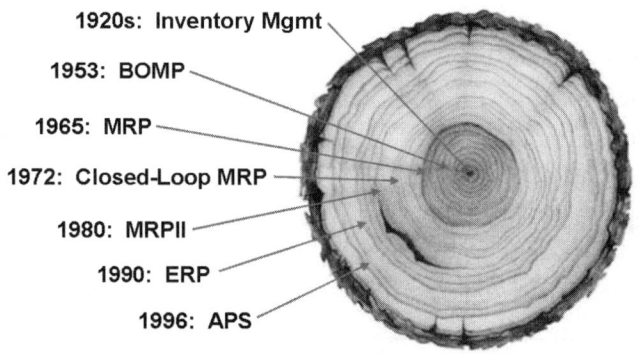

```
1920s: Inventory Mgmt
  1953: BOMP
  1965: MRP
1972: Closed-Loop MRP
  1980: MRPII
  1990: ERP
  1996: APS
```

Alternative Manufacturing Approaches

On a parallel path, during the same time as the previously described technological evolution, new ways of doing business have developed. Beginning in post-war Japan, Ohno, and Shingo launched what would later become known as the Toyota Production System. They recognized that inventory was a non value-added function. Creating inventory, stocking inventory, and controlling inventory was also non-value added. The Toyota Production System focused on improving the process so that inventory could be dramatically reduced.

The roots of this just-in-time or lean technique can be tracked back to Venice in the year 1104 according to Jim Womack, the well-known author of *Lean Thinking*. The Arsenal in Venice was established in 1104 to build war ships for the Venetian Navy. Over time the Venetians adopted a standardized design for the hundreds of galleys built each year to campaign in the Mediterranean. They also pioneered the use of interchangeable parts. This made it possible to assemble galleys along a narrow channel running through the Arsenal. The hull was completed first and then "flowed" past the assembly point for each item needed to complete the ship. By 1574 the Arsenal's practices were so advanced that King Henry III of France was invited to watch the construction of a complete galley in continuous flow, going from start to finish in less than an hour.

Dr. Womack further details the timeline of lean as:

▶ By 1765, French General Jean-Baptiste de Gribeauval had grasped the significance of standardized designs and interchangeable parts to facilitate battlefield repairs. Actually doing this cost-effectively in practice was another matter and required another 125 years.

▶ By 1807, Marc Brunel in England had devised equipment for making simple wooden items like rope blocks for the Royal Navy. He used 22 kinds of machines that produced identical items in process sequence one at a time.

▶ By 1822, Thomas Blanchard at the Springfield Armory in the U.S. had devised a set of 14 machines and laid them out in a cellular arrangement that made it possible to make more complex shapes like gunstocks for rifles. A block of wood was placed in the first machine, the lever was thrown, and the water-powered machine automatically removed some of the wood using a profile tracer on a reference piece. What this meant was really quite remarkable. The 14 machines could make a completed item with no human labor for processing and in single piece flow as the items were moved ahead from machine to machine one at a time.

▶ By the 1850s all of the American armories were making standardized metal parts for standardized weapons. Enormous amounts of handwork were required to get each part to its correct specification. This was because the machine tools of that era could not work on hardened metal. Instead they machined soft metal. The subsequent hardening process introduced warping of an unpredictable nature that had to be corrected by hand before parts would fit together. The expense was acceptable for military hardware but unacceptable for most consumer goods.

▸ In 1914 Ford finally got all of these strands of thinking to come together with advances in cutting tools and a leap in gauging technology. Many suppliers could then produce hardened metal parts which consistently fit perfectly in Ford's fabrication cells and on his final assembly line. This was the secret to truly continuous flow.

▸ By the late 1930s, the German aircraft industry had pioneered take time as a way to synchronize aircraft final assembly in which airplane fuselages were moved ahead in unison throughout final assembly at a precise measure (TAKT) of time. Mitsubishi had a technical relationship with the German companies and transferred this method back to Japan where Toyota, located nearby in Aichi Prefecture, heard about it and adopted it.

▸ By the early 1950s Toyota had integrated the idea of take time with Ford's ideas on continuous flow. Toyota added the critical dimension of flexibility to make high-quality products in wide variety in small batches with very short lead times.

Back in the United States, the late 1970s saw the emergence of Just-In-Time. Significant successes were found at early adopters such as Hewlett Packard. Quickly, manufacturing cost drivers began to shift from labor to materials as manufacturers focused on their core competencies. More parts were purchased rather than being manufactured in house. A few lone voices in the wilderness advocated this different vision of manufacturing. John Costanza began to evangelize Demand Flow™ manufacturing. John openly criticized the push philosophy behind the MRP systems of the day with his 'No MRP' buttons. Jim Womack further developed these ideas with his work in Lean. Dick Ling developed and advocated the idea of sales and operations planning to truly exploit capacity for profits—an idea only now seeing support from commercial software. Dr. W. Edwards Deming began his quality crusade work in the U.S. after his amazing success in Japan. His work there transformed the meaning of 'Made in Japan' from cheap, poor quality goods to the 'Lexus quality' standard for which all manufacturers currently strive. This work and the work of Dr. Walter Shewhart (Plan-Do-Check-Act cycle) was the foundation behind the popular Six Sigma improvement concept today. Motorola brought the concept of DMAIC (design, measure, analyze, improve, and control) into the mainstream as they used improved quality to improve their overall performance. In 1984, Dr. Eli Goldratt startled the world with *The Goal* his business book that was also a novel. (Or was that a novel that was also a business book?) This book introduced the breakthrough ideas called the Theory of Constraints. It taught the lesson that every business has a goal. To really succeed the constraints to achieving that goal must be identified and managed. How many forget this common sense to continually pursue common practice and suffer for it?

Early adopters of these emerging ideas used pilot projects to embrace these new business practices. The early results were nothing short of amazing. However, as quickly as the champion for that specific approach left to pursue new opportunities or companies were merged and acquired, these successful pilot projects quickly fell by the wayside. The early pilot improvements quickly deteriorated. Many of these new ideas espoused technology to be part of the non-value added historical baggage to be eliminated. Technology was an expense rather than being considered simply tools to help achieve and sustain positive change. These innovative approaches often failed to become common practice. The early benefits quickly dissipated leaving behind confusion as to why the new technique really failed.

Manufacturing Today

Currently there is a startling convergence of fundamental issues to create a disruptive force, the significance of which has not been seen since the advent of the industrial age. Rather than each geopolitical area having its own unique issues and problems, around the globe all industries are struggling with the very same competitive factors. This can be considered manufacturing's perfect storm.

▶ **Worldwide Overcapacity:** the productivity gains of established companies from operational improvement and incorporation of automation, combined with the addition of significant new capacity in Latin America, China, and Eastern Europe have resulted in a worldwide glut of manufacturing capacity. This coupled with the global energy crisis and the social and economic divergent views (NAFTA, the creation of the EU) has created a global focus for manufacturing like never before. No longer is the constraint internal capacity. Now manufacturing companies around the world have more capacity that they have business. Worldwide the constraint is in the external market.

▶ **Market Volatility:** new technology including the Internet has significantly reduced transactional friction. This has created a buyer's market. Constantly new patterns for sourcing and outsourcing are emerging. Market volatility is extending the physical supply chain while simultaneously compressing product lifecycles.

▶ **Customer Power:** access to information through the Internet has irrevocably shifted the global balance of power to the customer. Now, no longer is the sales person the first contact with a customer, the company's image is established in the virtual world. The product, price, quality, delivery, and service form the many dimensions that the customer demands simultaneously. Due to global overcapacity, if one manufacturer is not able to meet the customer's demand at the price the customer wishes to pay, the customer simply moves onto the next supplier. What is best in class now may be barely acceptable in the near future.

Worldwide, today direct labor is less than 10% of a manufacturing company's cost of goods sold. This is down from 60-70% just 50 years ago. Process improvement that focuses solely on improving labor productivity now yields insignificant benefits. Companies must learn how to compete on their ability to identify their unique capability. Then they must identify profitable opportunities in the marketplace that exploit that capability. In addition, companies must now respond more quickly than their competition. Lead time is now a great challenge. Expectations of months are now weeks, weeks are now days, and days are now hours. No longer is it possible for a company to compete simply on the product itself. A unique and complete value package must be offered. Services are now a critical part of the manufacturing company. The services can be wrapped around the product so that the customer can maximize their utilization of the product. Alternatively the service could necessitate the demand for the product. In either case, manufacturing companies must become service companies to survive.

There is only one way to establish lasting competitive advantage in this new reality. A mutually advantageous relationship is necessary with the customer and/or supplier. Simply competing for a customer's business on price alone will not sustain the business. Suppliers now must be an integral part of the process. Internally, the manufacturer must relentlessly compress the product and transaction lifecycles. The complex inventory centric iterative forecasting, planning, and push scheduling approach must be replaced. Now a more strategic planning process is supported by a quick response, demand-driven, lean manufacturing company. This agile capability is necessary all along the supply chain. To survive and thrive in this new world, a company must combine a vision of how their unique capabilities can be profitably exploited to provide value for their customers. Then clearly aligned business practices and supporting technology is necessary to make this vision a reality. While many similarities exist between companies, it is their uniqueness that provides the source of competitiveness. For each company, this future reality is unique and each company walks its path alone. *Theory H.O.W., How Organizations Could Work* provides a practical, pragmatic way to identify that unique direction and the insights on how to achieve that competitive advantage.

Understanding the Constraints—They Are Timeless

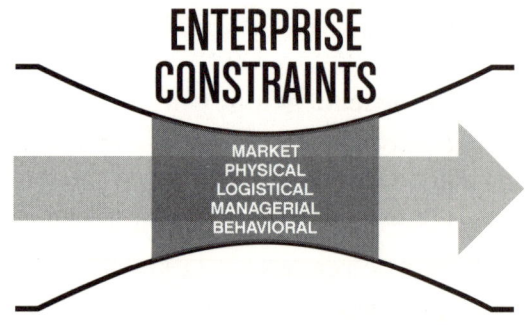

No matter how much the environment changes, the goal for sustainable profitability in manufacturing does not change. In the same way, the constraints impeding a manufacturer's ability to achieve that goal have also stayed stable. They are:

> **Market:** the market is a constraint when a manufacturing company possesses excess production capacity when compared to demand. The bottleneck for production is no longer internal. The company can produce all that the market demands. This does not mean that the company will not use a schedule for an internal constraint for the purposes of managing production. It does mean that this arbitrary schedule constraint is really capable of significantly more output—if only there was market demand for the product. A company in this position has the opportunity to develop a series of market offers. These different market offers segment the demand for its product by pricing and other factors.
>
> **Physical:** a physical constraint is a resource or process that limits the company's ability to increase throughput.

Companies just beginning the process of ongoing improvement will usually find an internal physical constraint. The steps to manage this constraint are to identify it, exploit it and then subordinate the rest of the enterprise to it. When this approach is done, the performance of the company improves dramatically (40-80% improvement) in a very short time. A physical constraint that is easy to overlook is a process constraint. This is not a single machine or station but rather an integrated process or function that is limiting the output of the company. A physical constraint is typically the easiest to identify and manage.

Logistical: a logistical constraint arises when the supply chain is considered. Logistical constraints can be the physical location of the company. This could be a long distance from its market or raw material. Logistical constraints can also be related to the product itself. For example, concrete parts would not be economical to ship by air or any great distance. Logistical constraints are identified when the linkages between the supplier to the business and the business to its customers are examined.

Managerial: managerial constraints reflect the formal and informal beliefs and convictions of the executive and management team. These constraints develop over a lifetime of individual experiences and overall organizational development. Managerial constraints can be difficult to identify.

To challenge them, test the individual's cultural norms and autonomic behavior. The managerial constraints derived from formal beliefs are frequently overlooked. The constraints from the informal beliefs may never be broken because of the difficulty of completely identifying them.

Behavioral: behavioral constraints derive from a company's culture and history. Every company evolves from its roots. Behavior changes only when measures change. Behavioral constraints are more easily identified by an outsider or new-comer to the organization. Having a new manager come into an organization and begin to ask "why?" quickly defines the behavioral constraints in the enterprise. The managerial and behavioral constraints are the most diffi-cult to change since these practices are most tightly aligned with an individual or company sense of self and identity.

The Requirement for Performance Driven Improvements

Improvements can only be made to those items that can be meas-ured. Conversely, if something cannot be measured then it cannot be improved. Improvement programs are intended to improve the bottomline. Billions of dollars have been wasted in improve-ment programs. At the end of the quarter or the end of the year, the bottomline has not improved at all. All measures are not cre-ated equal. Dr. Eli Goldratt, in *The Goal,* introduced the concepts of throughput, investment and operating expense as the three key measures for manufacturing. Building an entire perform-ance management system on these three measures ensures that improvements made will indeed generate bottomline perform-ance. When the measure of lead-time and delivery performance is added to those three, a performance measurement structure that is easily understood from the executive office to the shop floor is now possible. The most difficult constraints to manage, managerial and behavioral, are brought into the desired align-ment with these five elegantly simple measures. The goal is not to trade these measures off against each other and find an optimal point of performance. The desire is to improve all the measures simultaneously. When this happens, breakthrough results are realized on the bottom line as well.

During the reengineering craze of the 1980s it was not uncommon for companies to define all their "as-is" processes in a meticulously detailed fashion. This was followed by a similar time consuming process of defining the "to-be" processes. Then a project plan could be developed where a company detailed the migration from the "as-is" to the "to-be" over time through a series of improvement projects. This complex process involves a large number of people in the company and takes extensive time. This kind of project was a consultant's dream job. Doing this work allowed them to bill the same customer month after month. The unfortunate thing was that this "improvement" process can take months if not years. More importantly it yielded little, if any, positive bottomline results. In today's fast-paced environment, it is critical to be able to accurately identify the desired goal, the limiting constraint, factors impacting that constraint and options for exploiting that constraint until that constraint can be eliminated and the next one identified. Unlike the previous democratic improvement process where a voting process is used to define which processes will be targeted and improved, now those constraints must be identified with laser accuracy. Only then can a company hope to achieve a sustainable competitive position.

Summary

Remember that the source of sustainable competitive position comes from the 1% differentiating factor rather than the 99% of the business practices that are the same company to company. Manufacturing companies no longer can operate on the premise that tomorrow will look like yesterday. The future really looks little like the past. Those companies that possess a viable vision aligned with the right business practices and supported by technology will not only survive but thrive into the future, no matter where they are in the world. Some companies sit back and complain about unfair competitive practices domestically and internationally. They expect the government to step in and rescue them. These companies are in for a rude awakening. They will go the way of the large steel plant in Pittsburg or the American consumer electronics companies. Many no longer exist. The ones that do are different companies than just 10 years ago. Competition has never been fiercer, but at the same time opportunities have never been greater. Those companies that can identify their unique value to the market and then exploit it for competitive position will thrive in this new world.

A North American manufacturer may not be able to compete with cheap foreign imports on price. However, they have the distinct advantage of a location close to where the products will be consumed. This is an excellent example of a competitive advantage to be used to bring value to a customer. This manufacturer may be able to compete very effectively with a product having an extremely short product lifecycle, highly engineered products or items requiring rapid response. Possible options will be further explored in Chapter 4, The Theory H.O.W. Approach, and Chapter 6, Diagnostics Phase Dynamic Enterprise Characteristics.

The world of manufacturing has changed. A case can be made that the world of manufacturing has been changing for years. Recently the pace of change has been accelerating exponentially. The one thing that has not changed is the goal. Make money now and into the future. However, the world in which the manufacturing company pursues this goal is dramatically different. The traditional approaches that have been so successful for years no longer work. New ideas and creativity are necessary to discover how to achieve a sustainable competitive advantage. Being able to discern which of these ideas will lead to success is a success strategy in itself. *Theory H.O.W.* can help you separate the wheat from the chaff and put your company on the right road to the future. There is no time to make a mistake.

References

Lean Thinking : Banish Waste and Create Wealth in Your Corporation, Revised and Updated by Womack, et. al.

The Goal, Goldratt

TOC and its Implications on Management Cost Accounting, Smith, et. al.

Chapter 3
Getting Ready
for H.O.W.

Introduction

Many organizations jump right into projects without really giving them too much thought. They reach for the low easy targets for improvement. Then the quick victories are celebrated. The expectation is that significant improvement will continue at the same pace as the pilot programs are rolled out across the enterprise. Almost immediately the momentum slows and executive support for the project is withdrawn as positive returns can no longer be identified. Employees are disillusioned with the whole experience and vow never to make the same mistake to get involved again. This chapter will consider the preparatory steps needed to begin the Theory H.O.W. approach. By combining the strengths and benefits of Theory X, Theory Y, and Theory Z with *Theory H.O.W., How Organizations Could Work,* your organization can begin its transformation process on its best foot. Having a solid plan is necessary to gain support from all the employees who believe that this is just another fad that will quickly flash and die. Everyone needs the assurance that the journey has been well thought out and that all their hard work does actually make a difference for the company.

In the beginning of any improvement process, the low easy targets are always tempting. Commonly, improvement teams will harvest those early benefits and then call the project a success. In reality, success is when the improvement process becomes sustainable even through organizational changes as people move or leave.

Every organization and every individual has his or her own way of doing things and his or her own comfort zone or preference to how things should be done. We have all had the experience of "being in the zone" when things just click and good results happen. When we are out of our zone, it feels uncomfortable, frustrating and unfamiliar. Under pressure everyone will return to their comfort zone. In "Introduction to Type" Dr. Isabel Briggs Myers suggests that you can demonstrate this to yourself by writing your name twice on a piece of paper—first write with your dominant or favorite hand—and then again using your other hand. When using your preferred hand, you don't even think about how to write your name. You just do it—it comes naturally.

When using your non-preferred hand you probably did not have the same experience. It felt uncomfortable, it took longer, it was frustrating, and the results were terrible even though you worked harder at accomplishing it. Many people can actually write with both hands but usually not equally well. We use both our hands every day to do many tasks but we still tend to favor one over the other. Think about establishing an unfamiliar process by which the company will achieve substantial benefits. The team will feel the same way you did when writing your name with the "wrong" hand; they are working very hard and yielding substandard results.

Successfully getting a team down the learning curve so that this new way is now in their comfort zone is critical to success. Our challenge is to identify the comfort zones of the teams and the players early on so that we can leverage what is already comfortable to make the transition easier to what is uncomfortable.

H.O.W. to Get Organized

Choosing the right team leader and team can make all the difference. The best team leader is not necessarily the person with the biggest title and official power. Some of the best leaders are those who have no official title and no official power. What they do have is the trust and respect of the people around them. Having this person on your team, preferably as a team leader, is a great place to start the project.

Organizing Formal Teams

The project structure and organization is the framework by which the decision processes will be managed. However, your continuous

Figure 3.1 **Suggested project team structure**

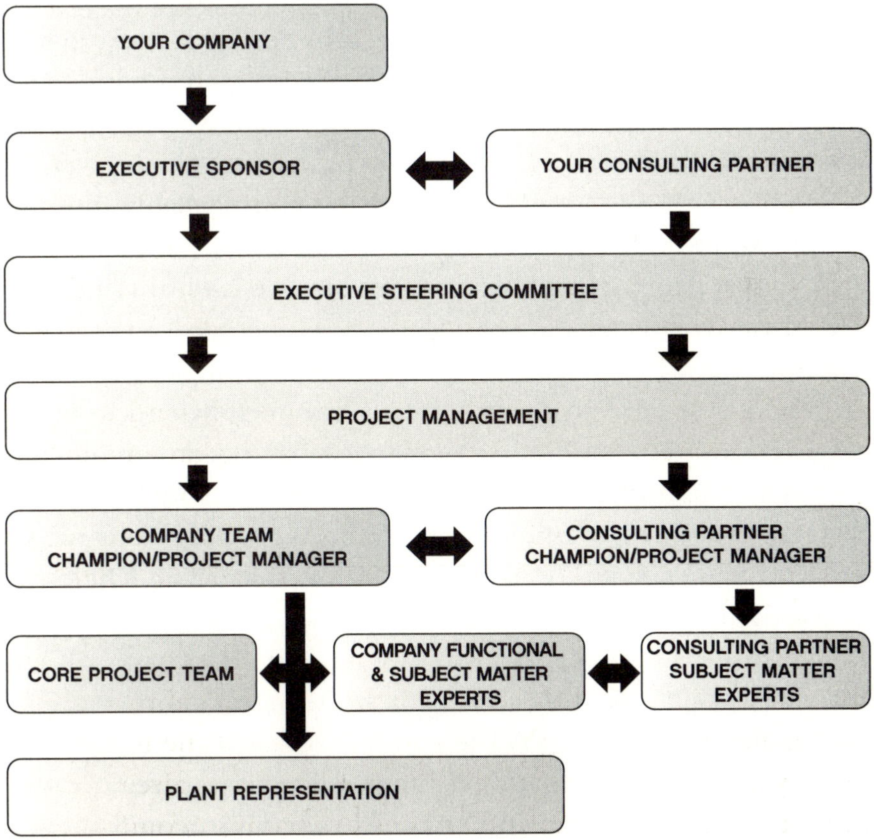

improvement organizational structure has to also fit into your current or transitional overall organizational structure to be successful. As your company introduces transformation ideas, integrated systems and new improvement changes to its business processes, the organization will encounter challenging issues requiring decisive resolution. These management issues are normal, and indeed necessary, as your company seeks to capture the inherent benefits of each new solution. The efficiency by which these issues are addressed and resolved will determine the ultimate success of the program. The most important thing when organizing teams is to clearly define the desired goal. Without this definition, the process can overtake the project. The goal becomes the team itself rather than accomplishing company bottomline results.

While watching a favorite football team, no spectator ever stops to review the roles and responsibilities of the players and specialty teams. Their performance will be criticized and judged as a team, not as individual players. Every player on every team knows exactly what needs to be done and how. It is all in their playbook. These teams understand that the team depends on all the members. It is not possible to have a star quarterback if there is a terrible offensive line or the receivers cannot catch. Only when the rest of the team does their job does the quarterback really show his potential.

Every person must know that they can depend on the other members of the team to do their job. Those members must know they can depend on everyone else. Remember that depending on the size of the company and the project not every role described in this chapter must be filled. Some of the roles may not be required until later in the project or may never be necessary at all. The project implementation plan will dictate the final necessary structure.

Role Clarification
Executive Sponsor
The Executive Sponsor provides the investment perspective and the desired strategic direction. Any issues arising that pertain to

Policy, Audit/Controls, Budget, and Scope are addressed at the sponsor level. These issues will ensure the benefits of the investment can be attained within the policy or strategic constraints of the business.

The Executive Sponsor should preferably be the number one cheerleader for change. In addition, this person must be at a sufficiently high enough level in the organization to foster change and make decisions. The sponsor must exude confidence and commitment about the need for change.

Project or Program Manager

The Project Manager provides guidance to the team and the single-mindedness of purpose and required focus. A successful project manager provides the glue to keep the team together and the motivation to bring about change quickly. An effective project manager should be a person with sufficient experience in the industry and who enjoys credibility within the organization to make this change. This person must also be a motivator, a mover & shaker, and someone not satisfied with the status quo. Desired personal skills include good communication, project management, and organizational skills. At times an outsider to the plant or company is necessary to have the needed objectiveness. However, if an outsider is used, this person then must have impeccable industry credentials as well as great depth and experience in this type of project. The Project Manager has probably the most difficult position in the process. Not only must they provide leadership to the team how it is needed and when it is needed but also the capability to communicate with the Executive Sponsor when additional assistance is required.

Steering Committee or Executive Team

The Steering Committee provides the management perspective to ensure the project is moving toward its objectives. This is an active decision body consisting of operational leaders capable of affecting organizational change. The Steering Committee is guided by a common understanding of the goals and resolves process issues of operational significance. This committee also deals with change management and resource issues. These often result from operational priorities conflicting with project demands. The steering committee then can formulate recommendations on issues requiring Executive Sponsor action. This team will most likely not agree totally on every issue. However, it is important to portray a unified front to support and encourage the necessary changes. Timeliness of decisions is critical to the overall process. The Steering Committee must be the grease in the wheels of change by supporting the improvement teams with timely decisions and leadership to make the necessary changes happen.

Team Leader(s)

The Team Leaders provide a valuable control perspective necessary to reconcile the interdependencies between the various functions of the business. This decision body comprises influencers who can convey to their teams the need for process change.

Team Leaders clarify cross-functional issues and present recommended options for Steering Committee resolution. These leaders drive day-to-day project execution and leadership for the team. Similar to the Project Manager, Team Leaders require a wide diversity of skills including:

- ▸ A change agent and driver.

- ▸ Good analytical abilities.

- ▸ Good people skills.

- ▸ Broad industry experience.

- ▸ Not afraid to escalate issues.

- ▸ Identify roadblocks to improvement.

- ▸ Focused on the goal.

Subject Matter Experts (SME)

The Quality Assurance and Subject Matter Experts provide specialized knowledge in key areas such as, project risk management, financial process analyses, and operational and organizational best practices. The Quality Assurance and Subject Matter Experts should be able to possess more extensive knowledge and experience in specific areas to support the team's efforts as well as possessing very good analytical and communication skills.

Functional Teams

The Functional Teams provide the expert operational perspective and institutional experience.

These teams derive detailed operational requirements and configure them, as business rules, into the solution. These individuals are the change agents needed for the company's transition to a new environment to realize the intended benefits of the investment. Participation in the teams may be full or part time depending on the focus of the specific team and the depth and breadth of the improvement action.

Technical Teams

The Technical Teams provide support from the technology perspective. These teams facilitate the implementation of new software and the underlying technical infrastructure. These teams also provide the insight and resources needed to build interfaces and conversions as well as architect the system to provide optimal access by end users.

Choosing Team Members

Selecting the best team members is essential to the success of a continuous improvement process and for the program overall. Each member has important responsibilities as technical experts, team leaders, and project heads. Not every good employee is a good team member candidate.

Serving on a continuous improvement team combines leadership ability, technical skills, some statistical knowledge, and the ability to communicate clearly and motivate employee curiosity.

Team members are the technical leaders and change agents. They implement the new principles, techniques, and tools. Successful team candidates generally share the following traits:

▶ Work well on their own.

▶ Work well in groups.

▶ Remain calm under extreme pressure.

▶ Anticipate problems and act on them immediately.

▶ Respect their fellow workers and are respected by them.

▶ Inspire others.

▶ Able to delegate tasks to other team members and coordinate their efforts on assignments.

▶ Understand and recognize the abilities and limitations of their fellow workers.

▶ Show a genuine concern for others, for what they need and want.

▶ Accept criticism well.

▶ Concerned about the current processes and results and they want to improve the system.

▶ Have the intelligence and interest to learn how to apply the different continuous improvement tools.

On the next page is a simple assessment tool that can help you determine the suitability of each person considered for the team. This form will identify the potential risks and holes that need to be filled when putting together a team to begin this process.

Figure 3.2 **Team Member Evaluation Form**

Rate each person being considered for the continuous improvement team on the following criteria, on a scale of 1 to 5 where:

5 = Excellent, 4 = Above Average, 3 = Average,
2 = Below Average, 1 = Unacceptable

Process and Product Knowledge	_____
Strong Statistical Orientation	_____
Knowledge About Your Organization	_____
Communication Skills	_____
Self-Starter, Motivated	_____
Open-Minded	_____
Eager to Learn About New Ideas	_____
Desire to Drive Change	_____
Team Player	_____
Respected	_____
Results Track Record	_____
Coaching / Mentoring Skills	_____
Interpersonal Skills	_____
Analytical / Evaluation	_____
Problem-Solving Skills	_____
Leadership Skills	_____
Strategic Thinker	_____
Basic PC Skills	_____
Financial Acumen	_____
Task / Execution Orientation	_____

Total _____

70 or above—excellent potential.
50-70—good possibilities, but consider other team members to comple-ment the weak areas.
Under 50—probably not a good idea.

Choosing a Good Change Agent or Consultant

Engaging the right consultant can make a big difference in the project. Consultants have previous experience in a variety of companies in your industry. The good ones provide an outsider's perspective but also understand and respect the internal company culture. Beware consultants that are inflexible or pedantic in their approach. This is a sure sign that they lack the expertise and experience to adapt to a new environment and apply concepts in a variety of situations.

The old adage "give a man a fish and he eats for a day, teach him to fish and he eats for a lifetime," applies to good consultants. A good consultant complements the team but is not the main resource on the team. Having a consulting firm come in and do the project is not only very expensive, but also yields poor results since the internal company resources are not committed to the change when the consulting team disengages. While this may seem to a be a great short cut to get the work done quickly, in the long run it actually takes longer and cost significantly more.

Other reasons to engage an outside consultant include:

▸ **Provide focus:** It is very easy to lose focus on a project when all the day-to-day issues continue to arise and demand the attention of everyone in the entire company. Having an outsider engaged can quickly bring the process back on track. This outside person provides a deadline by which activities need to be completed and when they need to be completed. Because of the expense of bringing this person in, the team will drive to complete its action items to that deadline.

▸ **Obtain tried and true methodologies:** Consultants possess experience in a variety of companies and exposure to a great deal of best practices. The successful ones have learned not only what works but how it works and why. Leveraging that knowledge saves time and effort internally.

34

▸ **Extra resources:** Any project adds workload to the company. To get over the additional workload hump consultants can provide the extra resources needed. This can be a costly solution, however, and should be done only when absolutely necessary. Turning the whole project over the consultants can be very tempting—and very dangerous.

▸ **Unbiased facilitation:** Since consultants do not have any political agenda in the company, they can provide an unbiased view and identify the political constraints inside the company better than any insider. A good consultant will ask the question that everyone knows needs to be asked but no one will take the risk to ask.

▸ **Mitigate project risk:** Any time a new process or territory is explored, having someone involved who has already navigated the waters will reduce the risk.

Some options for choosing a consulting partner are:

▸ **Independent consultant:** This person can serve as a full-time internal coach. This is usually an independent consultant that becomes temporarily an internal resource to the company. This type of consultant must have the highest and broadest level of expertise since there is only one individual engaged. The advantage is the development of a strong relationship and trust with this individual. The disadvantage is that if they do not have the strengths where necessary to complement the company's weakness, there are no other resources to draw upon. These people are also typically the most expensive on a per hour basis since they do have the breadth and depth of knowledge to stand on their own. Consider the total cost for the project weighed against the support to fully evaluate this option.

▸ **Major consulting firm:** The advantage of a major consulting firm is the breadth and depth of the resources available.

The disadvantage is that rarely are the most senior resources with the best knowledge base and expertise engaged on a day to day basis on your project. These companies hire less experienced people. This means they require more people on the job to gain the same breadth of experience. Many of them struggle to price at a level that is affordable for smaller companies. The advantage is that if someone on your project leaves their position for another company, the large consulting company has the depth of bench to replace that individual. Be aware that the people that sell the project are unlikely to be actually delivering the project. It is very common to have a senior person coaching and managing a much larger team of very junior people each with a very narrow focus of expertise.

▸ **Boutique consulting firm:** The smaller size of this firm provides a stronger relationship than possible with a major consulting firm but the breadth and depth of this firm is significantly limited as compared to a major consulting firm. However if the consulting team has the experience and expertise to resolve your problems and blends in well with your organization, this relationship can be both cost effective and beneficial.

▸ **Local consulting firm:** These are usually smaller boutique firms. The additional advantage is that the travel and living cost is significantly reduced.

▸ **State-sponsored consulting firm:** A plethora of very experienced resources are now available through the various states for small businesses. By checking the local Small Business Administration (SBA), you may discover some very competent resources at a very reasonable price.

When evaluating an outside consultant the following factors and questions should be considered:

▶ **Cost effectiveness:** This is not merely a price per hour, but rather what value is the consultant able to commit and for what price. A consultant with a higher price per hour may actually be less expensive because this individual requires less time to complete the project than a less experience consultant.

▶ **"ROCI"—Return on Consulting Investment:** When engaging a consultant there is an expectation of a positive return on this investment. Are the deliverables and expected return clearly defined? Is the consultant willing to put part of their fee at risk dependent on the success of the project? Remember that most consultants charge by the hour engaged so it is in their best interest to charge as many hours as possible.

▶ **Track record:** What projects have been done previously? What was that ROCI? How long has the consultant been in business? This includes their time as a consultant but also doing your type of project as a practitioner. Ask how many of their previous and most current customers can serve as references.

▶ **Project success and failure:** Any consultant that claims they have never had a failure is either a liar or they have not done multiple projects. Humans learn from their mistakes and problems. The best consultants are the ones who have learned from their previous mistakes. These are the people who can apply concepts to a variety of situations in a variety of ways rather than just having one way. Be wary of any consultant who has only one story or has only one expertise. These people are one trick ponies and if your problem happens to fit their one capability then your experience will be positive. If your situation falls outside their area of expertise, then you are going to be very frustrated and dissatisfied.

- ▶ **Clients:** Ask for a complete client list and not just the reference list. Ideally the client list reflects your industry and companies similar in size and scope.

- ▶ **People:** Ask to meet the actual people who will be assigned to your project. In large consulting companies, this option may not be available. Be aware of that. Given that the success or failure of your project relies on the people involved, insist that you meet and approve at least the project leaders. You are buying what someone knows and how they interact with your team's dynamics so it is critical that you know who that person is.

- ▶ **Culture:** Every company has its own unique culture. The consulting company culture including honesty, integrity, and customer service must all be consistent with your own company culture. Having a culture mismatch between both companies can create conflicts in the most difficult times of the project. Even the most successful project has difficult times.

Naming the Project

What's in a name? Shakespeare said that a rose by any other name would smell as sweet. In a transformation process, a name will communicate a message not only to the internal organization but also to the outside world. Calling this effort a project communicates that there is a beginning and an end. Calling this a process, communicates that the effort will be ongoing. Calling this a program communicates a more extensive impact than just a project. Do not name the process the same name as the software or other technology that may be used. The software is necessary but not sufficient for the overall effort's success. Similarly, how the effort is begun sends a strong message about the importance and the expectations of the senior management team. The visibility of the entire project in the company must match its significance.

Educate & Train the Team

Not every member of the implementation team needs to be a subject matter expert on all essential topics. The team members' skills must be aligned with the roles they will play as part of the project team.

The entire team will require education and training to be completely successful during the transformation process. Education is the awareness of the subject matter and how it fits together overall. Training provides the necessary skills to complete the tasks at hand.

The overall education and training must take into consideration the entire organization as a part of the company team.

Some of the critical skills needed include:

▸ **Business flow mapping:** This is necessary so the team can draw their supply chain and the connections between links of the supply chain. They will also need to be able to draw their current critical business processes as required.

▸ **Product flow diagramming:** Product flow diagrams will be required for each representative product family. These flows will also be used to determine which flow pattern exists at the company. The possible flow patterns are VAIT. These patterns are further described in Chapter 5, Static Enterprise Characteristics.

▸ **Value stream mapping:** This mapping process will help identify the constraints to flow and increased overall throughput.

Assessing the team's skills is a critical step and is frequently overlooked until a deficiency impacts the project. This assessment will identify the strengths and weaknesses of the team. The areas and skill sets are highlighted that are required to support the program in the most effective manner.

This assessment can include:

- ▸ What they have read.

- ▸ What courses, workshops, seminars attended.

- ▸ Other team experiences.

- ▸ Other transformation experiences.

- ▸ How long ago were these experiences.

Managing the Overall Process

When embarking on a journey of this significance, factors that must be considered are:

- ▸ **Project management and governance:** This area includes how the project will be run and how decisions and conflicts will be resolved. Any experienced project manager will have extensive background in this area.

- ▸ **Policy deployment:** The goal of this transformation is to change the current practices and business rules. This is a change in policy that must be deployed throughout the entire company. Policy deployment is a planning and implementation process that completely focuses the organization on a few key long term customer driven breakthrough objectives that are critical for the company's long term success.

- ▸ **Documentation:** Whether it is linking your vision statement and goals to measurable objectives for all team members or establishing work station instructions, it is extremely important that you provide the documents that support the process and continue to return value. Documentation is frequently something that is overlooked until too late. Memories are very short and it is critical that decisions and processes are well documented. Documenting the desired business direction, control, and processes is critical to companies of all sizes. The challenge with documentation is that these documents should be used and updated regularly. This means that the documentation should be easy to understand and practical. Good documentation is not just filed on a shelf or used as a paperweight. Good documentation aids with the training process and becomes an integral part of the new business practice.

▶ **Communication—"Sell, Sell, Sell:"** Many ways exist to sell the new ideas throughout the organization. Some of the most common are:

- Newsletter

- Email

- Intranet

- Direct voice mails

- Town meetings

In any case, formal lines of frequent communication are necessary. In the absence of real information, employees at the company will make up their own.

As your company begins the process of implementation, the organization will need to be constantly updated on the progress of the program. The executive committee provides the Implementation Team with direction and conflict resolution. The Implementation Team reports to the executive committee on the progress, results, and issues.

The program manager communicates to the team on the day to day activities. The company and consulting partner need to have frequent communications in order to keep the project on target. The entire organization as a whole needs to be constantly reminded as to the goals and direction of the program in order to remain focused!

Figure 3.3 **Communication flow process**

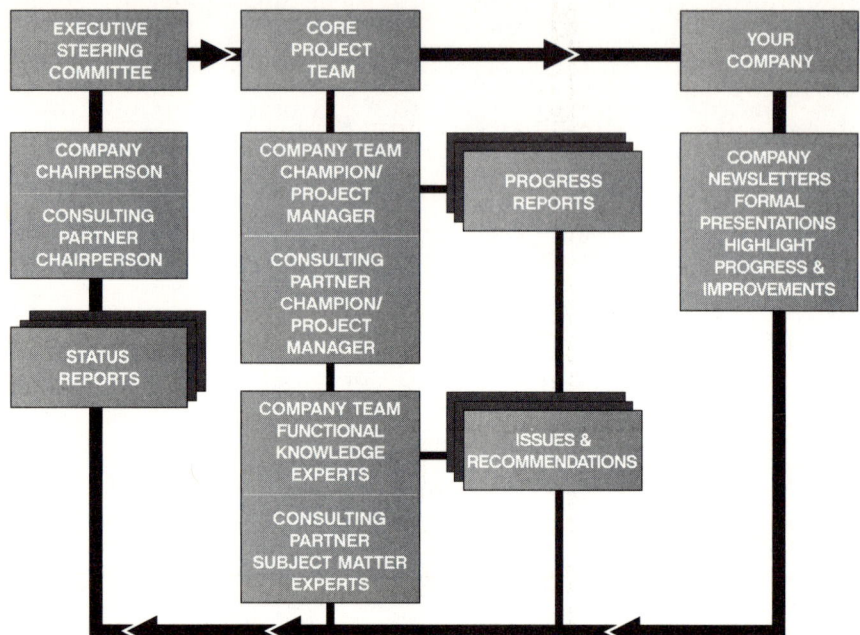

Celebrating Success

Whether it's spiking the ball after completing a short pass, pump-
ing your fist after making a long putt, or reducing the set up on
a critical machine by 15 minutes—it's important to celebrate the
win! This is a significant change for the company.

Establishing mile posts and celebrating when they are
achieved provides the motivation for the project team to continue
on its course. Remember that this is a transformation process
with no end. Celebrating success is necessary to continue that
momentum and keep the team motivated.

Summary

Theory H.O.W. will bring your organization to a variety of new
challenges and opportunities. As with any journey, it is necessary
to be prepared before setting out. This process not only brings
the early quick wins to the company but also establishes a long
term sustainable competitive advantage.

The organization of the team, the reporting structures, and the training and education are all critical success factors.

The current business environment is moving more quickly but taking the time to prepare properly at the beginning of the project will save a significant amount of time later.

References

Introduction to Type, Myers

Chapter 4
The Theory H.O.W. Approach

Introduction

In the classic story of *Alice in Wonderland,* as Alice faced a critical fork in the road she asked the Cheshire Cat for directions. The famous response is as applicable to businesses today as it was then to Alice. The road you take depends on where you want to go. If you do not know where you want to go then the road does not matter. This simple fact explains billions of dollars wasted on technology and process improvement. As firms strive to achieve competitive advantage, there must be a clear articulation of the goal. Although that seems so simple, establishing a clear goal can be as complex as the company itself. The goal provides the context and focus for both the technology and process improvement projects. Still, once the goal has been established, the road to achieve it can be fraught with challenges and difficulty. This chapter will explore the Theory H.O.W. holistic approach to help you begin the breakthrough process.

Archimedes on Fire

Archimedes said that if he could find the leverage point, he could move the world. Finding the leverage point in a company brings the focus to where improvements can be made that will bring direct benefit to the bottomline. Think of a two lane bridge over water. If you have ever had to contend with that in your daily drive, you know that the time to get over the bridge is directly related to the backup in front of that bridge. If additional lanes are built just in front of the bridge, simple logic would predict that it should take less time to get over the bridge since the miles of backup in front of the bridge have been reduced. However, common sense tells us that unless the lanes on the bridge are also increased, the time to get over the bridge will not change with additional lanes. In the same way, how many times in business is the financial case made for an improvement project or a technology purchase with exactly the same logic? A measure may accurately predict financial performance in an ongoing state. However, a project to significantly improve that measure may not result in significantly improved financial performance. Finding the real leverage point ensures that successful improvement projects or technology implementations will also dramatically improve the bottomline for the company. Think of Archimedes when considering any improvement project.

On the other hand, fire is the unavoidable consequence every time a fuel source, ignition, and oxygen are in the same place. If any of these three items is removed, then there is no fire. If anything else is added, then it is just extra. In the same way, a company can lead the market in financial performance when it combines a compelling vision, business policy and practices, and the necessary technology. This is clearly shown in the Theory H.O.W. approach. The term "Archimedes on Fire" comes from the combination of the focus on the real constraint of the business with the complete solution of vision, business rules, and information technology.

A company that focuses on a compelling vision and works only on the business policies and practices will discover that it is impossible to sustain the results and momentum of the initial pilot programs because the necessary technology is missing to

institutionalize these new processes. Many different schools of
process improvement thought
each seem to deny the neces-
sity of technology for the sustainable success of their
technique. Each zealot points
to the success of early pilots
but then will realize that there is
no large scale sustained rollout
available as an example. Appropriate
technology is necessary for the true integration of these improvement ideas into the day-to-day process.

A company that focuses only on vision and technology quickly discovers that significant resources have been expended to purchase and implement technology only to discover that there have
been little if any positive results on the bottomline. Companies
have spent millions of dollars on technological solutions only to
fail to show any solid return on that investment. Many software
companies are guilty of making the claim that if only the customer will purchase their software then dramatic improvements
will be seen in their business and their bottomline. Without
changing the appropriate business practices to utilize the technology, this is impossible. Microsoft® could make the claim that
if you purchased the latest version of Microsoft® Word you could
become a great author. If you are a poor writer before the purchase, simply purchasing the software will not make you great.
Why do so many people believe differently when it comes to technology for business?

Still other companies focus on the technology and business
practices only to discover the goal becomes how much technology can be bought and implemented. They realize that changes
are needed in the business practices to fit the program.
Unfortunately they don't consider how that implementation
project supports the company's overall vision and goals.

Consulting companies have attempted to work around this issue by providing "industry best practices" as a template for technology implementations. In the last decade, ERP (enterprise resource planning) implementations have used this strategy to reduce the implementation cost. Unfortunately since the project was not tied directly to the vision, only a small handful of implementations realized their business case. In addition, if these industry best practices become the general strategy for implementations then soon all companies in the same industry would have the same business practices. From where would competitive advantage come?

Only when there is a clear understanding of the goal can there be a context for the technology and business process improvements. Just like the three necessary conditions for fire, the three necessary conditions for breakthrough improvement are vision, business rules, and technology. "Archimedes on Fire" is one way to think of the combination of these three necessary conditions aligned with a focus on the leverage point for the company.

THE THEORY H.O.W. ZONES

The Vision Zone

The vision zone provides the focus and context for the entire company. This is very different than the traditional mission statement displayed at so many plants.

"We will be the world's premier provider of product X at a profit to ourselves, provide great customer service, be a great place to work and, be kind to the environment."

The time and effort that goes into the development of this kind of mission statement would be better spent on the golf

47

course. Many consultants have made a living facilitating this kind of statement and then further defining activities and actions until the overall strategic plan is the size of the New York City phonebook. Similar to that phonebook, the best purpose for this document is as a doorstop. Once a plan like this has been developed—at great expense—the document typically sits on the shelf never to see the light of day again.

The vision zone is not a dream or apparition but rather the foresight for the overall market and position of the company in that future. To quote Dr. Eliyahu Goldratt, "What is the goal?" What could and should be a simpler question to answer? If this simple question cannot be easily answered by the top management team, then how can alignment of activities, measures, and actions be possible? The answer to this question is much more than the simple answer of "to make money now and into the future." The practical vision is one that provides real direction to everyone in the company. The company must clearly define the vision for themselves. This view is for internal use only. The vision has nothing to do with what is communicated to the outside world. Establishing a vision is not a marketing effort. This is a serious internal strategic planning effort to define the desired view of future reality, as all activities should be driven by this vision.

To establish a practical vision, three deceptively simple questions must be answered by company executives. These three questions provide the foundation for the vision and mission of the company.

▸ Where will we be allowed to make a profit?

▸ What will be our value to our customers?

▸ What business designs will drive this profit and shareholder value?

When beginning this process, the most common statement used

by executives to explain their company is: "You don't understand, we are different!" Consultants will laugh at this statement because they see the strong similarity to the last five companies in which they worked. In the movie *City Slickers*, Curly, a curmudgeon of a cowboy, explains to Billy Crystal that the secret of life is one thing. Billy Crystal of course wants to know what that one thing is but alas Curly dies before he shares that secret. This is no different for a company vision. It is true that any company has far more similarities than differences to others in its industry. However, it is the difference that is the source of competitive advantage. What is that one thing? A compelling vision is a clear articulation of how the company will exploit that "one thing" that makes it different to provide value to its customers at a profit to itself. Remember that the future cannot be predicted from the past. The source of profitability is likely to be very different in the future than it is today. In just the past few years, companies have had to incorporate services around their product or develop services that necessitate the use of their product as a source for profits. No longer is it possible to compete simply on the product itself. Current technology quickly commoditizes products. This puts the company into a price based competitive position—not a sustainable competitive advantage.

A company's value proposition is that articulation of what is unique about the company and how it will provide value for its customers at a profit to itself. This value proposition is not a list of product features and functions but rather how the customer's business problem will be uniquely solved by the company. Remember that every customer cares only about its bottomline. The most common way to attempt to improve the bottomline is for the customer to ask for a lower price on products and services. It takes real creativity and thought for a supplier to uncover the real opportunities to create profit for a customer by leveraging its own capability. According to Dr. Eli Goldratt, the average executive would rather spend millions of dollars on technology than 20 minutes really thinking about a problem to uncover the real cause. Billy

Crystal did find out what the "one thing" was—but only after a lot of hard work and serious soul searching. He also realized that the "one thing" was also unique to just him!

Once a company expends the time and effort and understands that "one thing" and how to leverage it into something that solves a real problem in the market, then the appropriate business designs can be developed that support the overall vision. Since the source of competitive advantage is a win-win value for the company and its customers, then there should be an ongoing benefit for shareholders as well. To determine exact steps towards a sustainable competitive advantage, begin with the enterprise assessment detailed in this book and the workbook *Theory H.O.W. To* that defines both static and dynamic enterprise characteristics. Through this assessment process you can then discover where the opportunity is for greatest improvement and alignment.

The Technology Zone

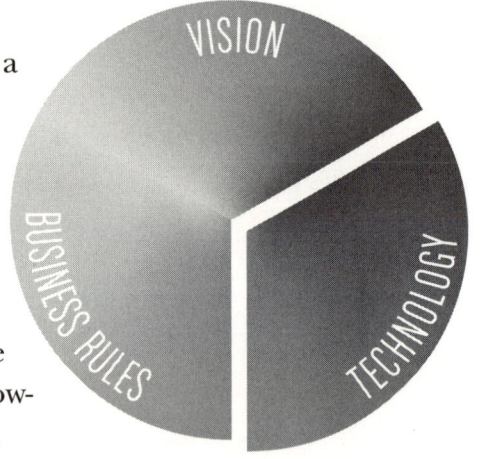

Technology can only provide a return on investment if and only if it addresses the constraint that is impeding a company's ability to reach its goal. Picking the right tools and implementing them to improve profits can be made much easier if the following six rules are kept in mind.

1. What is the main power of the technology? What does the tool allow you to do tomorrow that you cannot do today? For example, in the 1970s MRP (material requirements planning) was the latest technology. This planning tool had the capability to plan what materials are needed, how much needed to be ordered, and provided exactly when

they were needed. Prior to this technology, planning deep bills of material was almost impossible. Managing engineering changes on these complex assemblies required extensive manual effort. Even though this question seems so fundamental, it can be a difficult question for many software and technology companies to answer. They become so enamored with their technology that they forget the real goal is to solve business problems. Do not move onto question 2 unless you can answer this question.

2. What limitation does it diminish? Technology can only provide a return on investment if it addresses a limitation for the company. Any student of manufacturing flow quickly realizes that improving elsewhere than the bottleneck will not yield increased throughput for the plant. In the same way, putting technology or other tools into a business other than at the limitation will not improve overall throughput or generate positive bottomline impact. Conversely, when technology and tools are focused on the strategic limitation for the company, then significant bottomline return is very possible within a very short timeframe. Using MRP technology again as an example, the limitation addressed by the technology was that changes were very difficult to incorporate. Short product-lifecycle products required extensive manual effort to manage. MRP addresses those limitations with its powerful material calculation capability.

3. What rules helped us to accommodate the limitation? Every business that is an ongoing enterprise has somehow developed business practices and rules that have allowed the company to accommodate the limitation that the tools and technology are now intended to address. These business practices and rules must be identified. Otherwise, when the technology is implemented the return on investment will not be realized since the old business practice or rule is still in place. For MRP,

companies needed to change the business rule that every part should be in stock or on order all the time. Being comfortable having no parts on the shelf and trusting that the MRP system would release an order with sufficient lead time such that the part will arrive in time for use was a big obstacle in this transition. Prior to MRP, companies used an order point system which had everything on the shelf all the time. The minimum safety stocks were used to cover for the lead times to order and the variability of demand. Turning this planning function over to a computer system that did not carry the same level of inventory was a very difficult thing to do. You can see the conflict when the cost justification for the MRP system was a significant reduction in inventory.

Another example of challenging business rules is the speed with which modern ERP systems can calculate a material plan. In the old days, MRP was run once a week since it took so long to complete. Now ERP can calculate the material and capacity plan in near realtime. However, more than 90% of the companies using these modern systems still plan materials once a week. This is because the planners are still using the same techniques and rules they did under MRP system. The possible benefit of the ERP system to provide suppliers with near realtime visibility of demand requirements is not possible since the old business rules are blocking that possibility.

4. What rules should we use now? To fully exploit the technology, the appropriate business rules must be developed to replace the current rules in place to accommodate to the limitation. This means challenging the status quo and traditional practices. In the previous example of the transition from MRP to ERP, this could mean allowing the computer to automatically plan and communicate changes to suppliers. When approached with this idea, planners will quickly respond that their manual interven-

tion is needed because the input data are not that accurate. This accuracy is required to allow the planning process to occur automatically. However, putting statistical control limits on the transaction size and frequency will provide feedback to the planner of those items that are not accurate so they can be fixed. Soon the material plan takes on the same level of control as any process controlled by statistical process control. This ensures that the significant items or errors are managed without getting lost in the trivial items or issues.

5. In light of the change in rules, what changes are required in the technology? As described in the first section of this chapter, there is a synergy between technology and business rules. As the technology changes, the business rules must change to exploit the technology's new capability. Similarly, as experience is gained with the new technology and it is leveraged to further benefit in the company, changes are needed in the technology to further support newly developed business practices. This should not be confused with modifications to the technology to fit the old business rules. These are changes to technology to support desired new business rules and practices. A good example of this is the advent of e-commerce. When companies started to realize the potential of the Internet there was a desire to extend their ERP systems to the Internet. Customers could then enter their orders and get a delivery commitment in real-time. Significant technical changes had to be made in the company's systems to develop this direct linkage.

As systems became more connected, then companies could be even more creative in their product offerings with this direct communication to customers. This closed-loop improvement process continues as long as there is a constraint to the achievement of the company's desired goal.

6. How to cause the change? Most people believe that change is difficult and that people will resist change. People will always resist change they don't understand and don't support. People however will not resist change when it is in their self interest. Think of giving a person $10 million. This creates an incredible change for that person and their whole family. However, what person would not snap at the chance to get $10 million with no strings attached? This is an extreme example but it does demonstrate the point that people are very comfortable with change when it is in their best interest. A successful proven approach to change is described in the next section on business rules.

The Business Rules Zone

The business rules zone brings the focus and insight to your current reality. Business rules can be formal or informal. When new employees start at your company, their training and orientation is all about your business rules. These people could be the world's experts in their specialty but they still need the specific context about your company to be effective. This zone includes the definition of who you are as a company, what business are you in, what your position is in the market and the supply chain, and begins the process of defining of what you could be doing. The business rules zone compares the internal definition of the product, the manufacturing process utilized for that process and the market position for that product. A misalignment among these three creates an internal friction within the organization that may be difficult to identify as to its cause. When the three are aligned, there is a noticeable streamlining of the overall business processes. The identification of this alignment is covered in the next chapter, Static Enterprise Characteristics. In this section you will begin the journey of examining your current reality and the underlying conditions that cause that reality.

THE THEORY H.O.W. ZONE INTERACTIONS

Vision–Technology Interaction

As described previously, the Theory H.O.W. approach recognizes the strong interaction between the three necessary conditions required for breakthrough improvement. We will take these interactions in pairs to explore the transitions and pitfalls. The relationship between vision and technology is where the current reality is transformed into the desired future state. Software companies traditionally try to dominate the interaction between vision and technology. In the go-go days of ERP and APS (advanced planning and scheduling) systems, the software salesperson skillfully painted a desirable vision and then tied it to the features and functions of their product. For example, ERP salespeople discussed how business decisions could be made more quickly and accurately with the real time access to critical business information. APS promised to keep all capacity operating at peak efficiency all the time. Surely if everything is busy making more products, then the company would be more profitable? Right? These skilled salespeople then showed how their black box scheduler could optimize hundreds of bottlenecks instantly as well as rescheduling any disruption at the blink of an eye. This compelling demonstration sold many software seats and made many salespeople very rich. Unfortunately there are very few cases of companies utilizing this software that can really demonstrate a positive bottomline impact. There is no correlation between the attempt to keep all resources busy all the time and the business making more money.

Once the vision has been developed, it is then necessary to develop detailed plans to execute that vision. There are three supporting concepts to execute the vision properly: strategy, tactics, and tools.

Strategy
The strategy is more specific than the vision and should be stated in S.M.A.R.T. terms.

▶ **Specific:** The strategy must reflect a specific key market condition or competitive element that needs to be addressed to achieve the vision. This should be the limited factor impeding the company's ability to achieve that vision. Remember the two lane bridge. Improving other than at the constraint will not get the company closer to its desired state.

▶ **Measurable:** Keeping score is a innate human need. We all want and need to know how we are doing against other people and against our own previous performance. An effective strategy clearly defines not only the activity but also the measure of success. Are you attempting to reduce the backup at the bridge or get more cars over the bridge? Remember that what you measure is what you will get so it is critical to establish the measure to get the desired results.

▶ **Attainable:** The process described in Chapter 8 on the six layers of resistance to change will help the team believe that the goal is attainable as well as provide great insights on how the process will work exactly. While the vision is a very big, hairy, audacious goal, the strategy must be attainable within a specific timeframe.

▶ **Realistic:** Asking a group of people to rollout a sophisticated statistical process control plan but who do not have the math skills required to balance a checkbook is not realistic.

Not only must the strategy be attainable but given the current resource constraints, people, and market, the strategy must also be realistic. The group must be willing to strive for the goal.

▶ **Time Driven:** A sense of urgency is needed for the strategy. Remember this vision is what will allow the company to be competitive now and into the future. Any month, week, or day that goes by without embracing this strategy is a significant opportunity lost.

Tactics

Tactics are a method of employing resources to achieve a goal. Tactics are focused short-term actions that support the overall strategy. These are very specific actions needed to put the strategy into play. Think of tactics as the mile markers on the road defined by the strategy. This is the detailed project plan that the project team will follow. Useful tactics identify the vital few specific actions required to achieve the strategy rather than comprehensively listing the useful many ideas that can come from the planning process. The Theory H.O.W. approach helps identify these vital few tactics.

Tools

Tools in this context are a combination of technological tools and business-process improvement tools. The business process improvement tools are further described in the section in this chapter on business rules-technology interaction. The technological tools can be hardware, software, middleware, infrastructure, the Internet, or any combination of these. Innovation in technology provides a company the opportunity to explore new business opportunities and provide new value propositions to its customers. Beware of falling in love with a specific technology. This can become like a hammer looking for a nail. The right tool for the right job makes the job significantly easier. Remember that significant bottomline return is possible when the rules in the previous technology section are carefully followed.

The Theory H.O.W. assessment in later chapters will help isolate which technological tools may be the first for possible examination and implementation.

Vision—Business Rules Interaction

The interaction between the desired vision and the necessary supporting business rules is the mandate to change the current approach for the company. The static enterprise characteristics described in Chapter 5 provide the context for that change. This side of the circle is the place for breakthrough ideas and concepts. However, without technology to systematize the new thought process, slipping back to the old way of doing things is far too easy. When new concepts and ideas are introduced, a pilot approach can be used to test the idea. For good ideas, these pilots are successful and the team shows progress against the desired measures. However, even though the pilot was a great success, the company may not roll out these ideas on a large scale since the manual effort to make the pilot work is not scalable in the company. It is important that not only is there a strong vision but also the ability to execute that vision operationally.

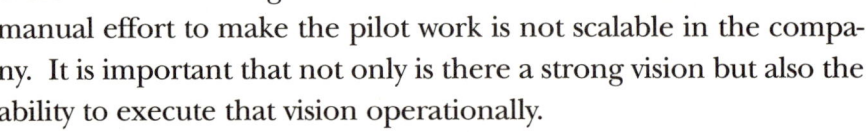

To do this, a number of steps are necessary and to begin this process:

▶ Assess the capabilities of the current operational methods including systems, organizational structures, costing methods, supplier relationships, etc. This provides a current profile of all key business attributes.

▶ Evaluate the existing culture/values of the organization(s). Is there openness to new ideas and processes?

▶ Evaluate current performance measures of the organization(s). Do they drive the desired behavior?

▶ Assess the products and services being offered to customers. Does the customer really value the items where the company is putting its efforts?

▶ Evaluate all your enterprise supply-chain operations and flow characteristics.

Please see Chapter 5 on Static Enterprise Characteristics and Chapter 6 on Dynamic Enterprise Characteristics for more detail. This process is also further defined in the *Theory H.O.W. To* workbook.

Business Rules–Technology Interaction

As stated previously, there is a closed-loop continuous feedback process between business rules and technology. In this section we will look at not only the technology but also the tools that can be used to speed that iterative loop. Further detail about this implementation strategy can be found in Chapter 8, Implementation Plan. A variety of tools can be used to identify where the opportunity areas may lie in the operation. These current tools are used to support the current process. Some of the tools that may be in your toolbox include:

▶ Theory of Constraints

▶ Lean/Flow Techniques

▶ Six Sigma

▶ Business Process Analysis

> ▸ Process Flow Diagrams

> ▸ Value Stream Mapping

> ▸ Fishbone Charts and other problem solving techniques

A very wise man, William Milliron, advises, "Remember that choosing the right tool for the right job makes that job much easier. Choose the wrong tool and you will fight it every step of the way." Completing the diagnostic phase will help you identify which are the right tools for your company. The improvement and implementation phases describe how to incorporate them into your overall project plan. The same advice holds true here as it does in the technology zone. Be careful about falling in love with a specific improvement technique. The process can easily overtake the project.

Summary

The Theory H.O.W. approach addresses all three necessary conditions—vision, business rules, and technology. By bringing together these three necessary components and focusing on the leverage point for the business—Archimedes on Fire—a roadmap is now clearly visible for an enterprise to achieve its goal. Managing this kind of substantial change can be a challenge but when each of the layers of resistance to change is addressed, the change is significantly easier and the desired goal can be achieved.

References

Attitude is Everything, Meyers

Chapter 5
Static Enterprise Characteristics

Introduction

Like each person, every company possesses a unique combination of characteristics. No two people are identical and no two companies are completely identical. Each has a personality based upon tradition, cultural biases, competitor profiles, market demands, and leadership style. As described in the vision zone in Chapter 4, competitive advantage is derived from that uniqueness. However, at the same time, companies can share many similar characteristics in the same way as people share common personality traits and reaction to stress. A leopard cannot change its spots nor a zebra its stripes. In the short term a company cannot change inherent characteristics that define its culture, approach to the market, and competitive position. These are static enterprise characteristics. However, a leopard can learn to hunt different game and a zebra can discover different watering holes and grasses upon which to feed. The process of ongoing improvement in a company provides the opportunity to quickly change these dynamic enterprise characteristics in response to changing market conditions and competitive forces. By understanding the static and dynamic enterprise characteristics separately and then how they reinforce or conflict, a company can certainly gain insight into possible breakthrough competitive strategies.

Static Enterprise Characteristics (SEC)—Definition

Static enterprise characteristics (SEC) describe specific attributes which define the core beliefs, culture, structure, and approach to the market, which under normal conditions do not change as the organization implements continuous improvement strategies. The static enterprise characteristics

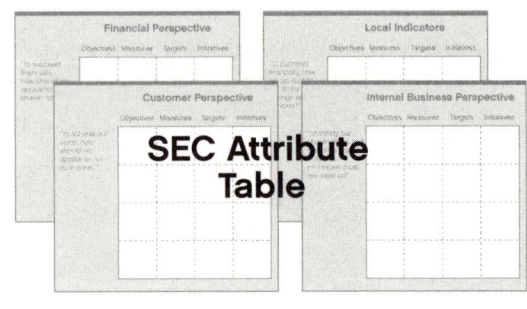

are a result of the evolution of the organization in its market through its years in business. Static enterprise characteristics are not typically the result of a single executive, but rather the accumulation of all executives resulting in the evolution of the company. These attributes can enhance or conflict with a desired competitive position.

Static enterprise characteristics are the foundation for sustainable competitiveness. When these attributes are in alignment with the desired competitive position, then a company expends less energy and resources to achieve its goal. When they are in conflict, then this friction requires additional effort and resources to overcome. Breakthrough thinking is not possible. Too much energy is expended maintaining a steady state. Continuous improvement programs are started and then quickly fizzle. Breakthrough results are impossible. By understanding the static enterprise characteristics, an executive can begin to identify possible breakthrough competitive opportunities or at least understand the real cause of higher levels than expected for resources due to the misalignment of the competitive strategy with the business infrastructure.

ENTERPRISE REQUIREMENTS PROFILE

Industry Type

The overall industry in which the enterprise company competes is the first level of understanding in the SEC profile process. The attribute table below describes in detail five different industry types.

Figure 5.1 **Static Characteristic Attribute Table—Industry Type**

	SERVICE INDUSTRY	ENGINEERED PRODUCTS	HEAVY PROCESS	DISCRETE PRODUCTION	MIXED MODEL
DISTINGUISHING CHARACTERISTICS	Revenue comes from non product activities	Highly specialized products that are typically built only once	Continuous flow Asset intensive Batch flow	Products are built more than once Output can be counted in unique units	Combination of different types (discrete, process, engineered, service)
MAJOR MANAGEMENT CONCERNS	Consistent quality of the service Hire the best people Retain trained personnel	Deliver products on schedule at the projected cost Retain talented engineering talent Keep engineers consistently busy	Minimize changeovers Keep equipment fully utilized building product Control maintenance costs	Efficient production Manage bottlenecks resulting from changes in product mix Increase flexibility	Manage the complexity of the overall process
TRADITIONAL STRATEGY	Hire and fire personnel in response to market demand	Assign multiple projects to an engineer to keep all projects moving forward	Continuous 24-hour operation with minimal setups to maximize efficiency	Minimize cost by reducing labor and improving overall efficiency	Departmentalize operations for accountability
SOURCES OF PROBLEMS	Mismatch of timing of resource availability to customer's demand expectation	Product lead time exceeds the customer's expectation. Frequent cost and schedule overruns	Customer demands higher variety in products than can be made economically	Lead times that exceed customers expectations Forecasts are highly inaccurate High variety of product mix	Critical synergy is lost between different departments due to inherent differences

▶ **Service industry:** The service industry has a very difficult problem because inventory cannot be stockpiled in advance of the customer's requirement. The service industry is a people business and people are far more difficult to manage than machines. Having the right people, in the right place, at the right time, with the right training, and the right motivation to satisfy the high expectations of the customer can seem like Mission: Impossible. An example of this industry is field service or distribution.

▶ **Engineered products:** Similar to the service industry, engineered products is a people business. Having the right people in the right place, doing the right thing is a real challenge. This is more difficult in engineered products because the skill level of the people is very high. Engineers are generally required since each product is complex and may never be built again. The goal here is to keep all these people working on value added projects. Invariably the portfolio of projects is never timed to be a great match for the availability of the engineers. The engineering department is a significant cost for the company and letting them stand idle is not desirable. Managing multiple projects is commonplace. Long lead times, in months or years, are a characteristic of this industry. Examples of this industry are companies making bridges and satellites.

▶ **Heavy process:** This industry is the most asset intensive of any industry. Fixed asset value can easily be more than three times the annual revenue. The heavy process industry employs relatively few people when compared to the overall space. The simple fact is that the enterprise makes money when the equipment is running. Conversely when the equipment isn't running, the financial loss is significant.

Changing equipment over to manufacture different products or breakdown on the equipment consumes valuable production time. To improve the desired overall efficiency, set ups and maintenance are carefully managed to the lowest point possible.

▶ **Discrete production:** This industry is more labor intensive than heavy process but not as much as the service industry or engineered products. The equipment is more generalized than the heavy process to enable a company to produce a wide variety of different products. Forecasting this product mix is a big challenge. Even though there is usually common raw material, the other details of each product must be thoroughly planned and synchronized. The skill level of the labor is not as extensive at the engineered products, but the company still attempts to keep everyone working on value-added activities. Several different approaches have evolved to manage discrete production, including a resource-centric structure like a job shop or a flow structure like an assembly line.

▶ **Mixed model:** A very common method is to mix and match a number of approaches in response to unique market conditions. For example, a company may use a heavy process approach to make a component that is finished in a discrete environment in a wide variety of ways. Or, the engineered products could be prototypes that eventually will be produced on a discrete line. The mixed-model approach brings the strengths and challenges together of each of the combined approaches making it more difficult to manage.

Demand Profile

The demand profile defines how orders are received for the products. Repetitive orders can be standing orders that are

Figure 5.2 **Static Characteristic Attribute Table—Demand Profile**

	REPETITIVE ORDERS	UNIQUE ORDERS	SEASONAL CYCLE	PRODUCT CYCLE	INDUSTRY CYCLE
DISTINGUISHING CHARACTERISTICS	Blanket orders Minimum number of internal customer service reps	Each order specifies the configuration of the product, price, and timing	Demand varies by the time of year in a repeatable manner	Product demand varies due to the product lifecycle (i.e. model years)	Product demand is cyclical based on the overall industry cycle (i.e. aerospace)
MAJOR MANAGEMENT CONCERNS	Keeping track of the blanket orders including the outstanding balance and renewal date Simplifying the shipment and payment process	Ensuring that there is a common understanding of requirements with the customer (configuration, price, and timing)	Ability to predict the cyclical effect soon enough to respond effectively	Ability to predict the cyclical effect soon enough to respond effectively	Ability to predict the cyclical effect soon enough to respond effectively
TRADITIONAL STRATEGY	Stock inventory in response to forecasted demand	Products are built to precise customer requirements	Forecast the cycle and promote the product to hit the expected demand	Forecast the cycle and promote the product to hit the expected demand	Forecast the cycle and promote the product to hit the expected demand
SOURCES OF PROBLEMS	Frequent ordering drives up replenishment costs and may consume significant profitability	Changes occur in configuration during the production process	The forecast can have a high error and the resulting promotion can significantly reduce profitability	The forecast can have a high error and the resulting promotion can significantly reduce profitability	The forecast can have a high error and the resulting promotion can significantly reduce profitability

repeated on a regular basis like delivering shop supplies or routine parts on a weekly or monthly basis. Unique orders come at any time and specifically define the configuration, price, and timing of the desired product. Cyclical demand can be affected by the time of year, the overall product life cycle, or the industry as a whole. Each of these patterns is very different and has a significant impact on how to manage the overall process.

Fulfillment Approach

The fulfillment approach describes how the production operation will deliver the customer demand. This can be thought of as a continuum from the highly technical engineer-to-order-approach where significant engineering work is required before even the first product can be built to the build-to-forecast-approach where the product being built has few, if any, configuration differences.

To better understand the fulfillment approach, the relationship between the volumes produced by the company is compared relative to the variety produced. An interesting diagonal has evolved where most companies are clustered in order to compete effectively. This position on the diagonal is the optimal position in terms of production cost and responsiveness. Movements from that competitive diagonal can either be a competitive advantage for the company or a disaster. According to Terry Hill in *Manufacturing Strategy*, this can be represented in the following matrix.

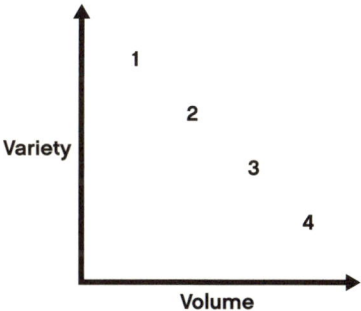

This relationship shows an inverse relationship between variety and volume. In general, as the product volume increases the variety tends to decrease.

Engineer-to-Order: Position 1

Position 1 of the volume/variety matrix is a company that produces a very high variety of products, but in very low volume. This can mean that a single product may be developed, planned, and produced once and never produced again. These products or deliverables are typically managed as unique projects. A project-driven company competes in the market based on the wide variety of products that it can produce utilizing the same resources. This type of company uses some computerized-planning system for determining what needs to be ordered and when. In addition, this organization will normally use a project-management system to determine the critical path for the activities of the project. The tools of the project-management company also include PERT (program evaluation review technique) and Gantt charts. These tools can provide the expected finish date once the start date is determined using forward scheduling. For each task in the scheduling network by using forward scheduling, the earliest a task can start is calculated. Or, given a desired completion date, the suggested start date can be calculated using backward scheduling. Backward scheduling determines the latest each task can start. In the process of scheduling all the required tasks, some tasks have a difference between early and late start or early and late finish.

When planning material to be available to begin a task, the difference between early and late start is significant. The question quickly arises about when the material should be available; in time for the earliest possible start or hold off investing that capital in inventory until the last possible minute? The project-type company must decide and establish the material policy for ordering needed materials choosing to be available at the early start, late start, or average start date. In most companies of this type the policy is to have the materials available at the earliest possible start date since a project-driven company's cost is typically driven most from the resources utilized rather than the materials. These resources are usually the constraint to the company delivering a higher level of output. Having a resource idle because materials are not ready or available can cause a great financial loss since this resource's capacity cannot be regained once it is lost.

Make-to-Order: Position 2

A make-to-order company competes in the market by providing a wide variety of products in the shortest lead-time possible. In addition to common raw materials, all products in a make-to-order company tend to go through similar operations. This type of manufacturing facility is generally capital intensive with general-purpose equipment that can accomplish a wide range of processes. An example of this kind of business is a machine shop making sheet metal parts for many customers. The operations used can include punching, forming, deburring, plating, and assembling. Almost an infinite number of finished goods can be produced from these basic operations. To effectively compete in the market, the make-to-order manufacturer tends to focus its marketing in one type of industry such as aerospace and defense, medical devices, or computer parts, etc. The constraint for growth in this type of company is typically knowledge of the market, the unique customer demands, and potential distribution channels and other routes to market rather than production capability. The cost of adding additional distribution channels is significantly more expensive than adding production capability.

The inventory strategy in this organization is to typically purchase a safety stock of the commonly used raw materials so that the overall response time to the customer can be reduced. Customers tend to order what they want at the last possible minute. Design changes after the order is placed are not unusual. Normally, relatively few raw materials are used in the normal course of business. The investment required in safety stock to shorten the response time is not all that significant. Another competitive strategy is to standardize the manufacturing processes to use common sizes of raw materials. Rather than using the size of material that provides the best material utilization, the company may standardize on sizes of raw material that are easily obtainable. Purchasing standard-size stock material prevents having to stock safety stock inventory since these standard sizes are normally in stock at the supplier. In addition, these standard-size materials are typically less expensive on a square foot basis. However, it is true that more of the material will be wasted than if the best-fit material was purchased. The savings in material cost and inventory cost can far outweigh the material utilization benefit. Understanding what the best solution is for the company as a whole must consider the cost of the wasted material, the inventory carrying cost to stock special material, the less-expensive stock material, the competitive position for the company with respect to lead-time response, and many other factors that impact the overall cost. This final decision is dependent on many factors and must be considered from an overall competitive position for the enterprise. The capacity strategy usually focuses on maintaining aggressive cross training with the operators so that they can operate a variety of machines. This enhances the overall flexibility of the enterprise and could lead to a market advantage.

Assemble-to-Order: Position 3

In the assemble-to-order company, the customer is provided with more product variety than the make-to-stock company if they are willing to wait a small amount of time. Typically manufactured and purchased parts are common to many assemblies; each assembly is made up of a series of options. Even though all the parts may be available, if there is no capacity with which to assemble, the product will not be available when expected. The assemble-to-order company is well suited to the expectations of customers for mass customized products on demand. The challenge is having the right building blocks available from which to make the final product.

Build-to-Replenishment/Build-to-Forecast: Position 3 & 4

Make-to-stock companies typically ship to customers on demand. The customers are not willing to wait very long for their needs to be fulfilled. They expect the products they want to be on the shelf, typically in a retail environment. Since manufacturing has to build products in advance of customer demand, the manufacturing schedule is typically driven by a demand forecast. Actual customer demand then consumes this forecast. In a build-to-replenishment strategy, more inventories are held in a buffer at the customer's location. When this buffer is depleted under a certain quantity, then additional materials are shipped to the buffer.

Figure 5.3 **Static Characteristic Attribute Table—Fulfillment Approach**

	ENGINEER-TO-ORDER (ETO)	MAKE-TO-ORDER (MTO)	ASSEMBLE-TO-ORDER (ATO)	BUILD-TO-REPLENISH (BTR)	BUILD-TO-FORECAST (BTF)
DISTINGUISHING CHARACTERISTICS	Sell capabilities rather than specific product	Only produce when product is sold	Specific options to choose from Product is assembled on demand from stocked components	Product is built to a forecast and kept in finished state to be shipped from the warehouse at the demand signal	Product is built to a forecast and kept in stock until sold
MAJOR MANAGEMENT CONCERNS	Design, build and deliver product to specification on time and on budget	Ability to produce and ship within time limitations	Having the right component inventory in stock and the capacity to assemble and ship on time	Forecast accuracy Finished goods inventory Accurate information from the customer buffer	Forecast accuracy Finished goods inventory Warehouse space
TRADITIONAL STRATEGY	Assign multiple project to engineers to improve efficiency	Ensure all resources are kept busy with sufficient work in process	Forecast sufficient components to meet any customer demand	Forecast sales and monitor the inventory at the customer site	Forecast sales
SOURCES OF PROBLEMS	Engineers switching from one project to another	Bottlenecks cause large inventory piles in front of some resources	Forecast inaccuracy	Forecast inaccuracy	Forecast inaccuracy

Distribution Approach

Distribution is necessary to get the product to market. As in previous static characteristics, there are a few choices. Product can be shipped direct from the company to the end consumer. Alternatively, the manufacturer may use a distribution network to consolidate demand. Still other manufacturers may use a mixed-model approach to get their goods to market. Factors to be considered when selecting a distribution approach is the cost of distribution and logistics, need or desire to have direct contact with the customer, product pricing, and channel management issues.

Figure 5.4 **Static Characteristic Attribute Table—Distribution Approach**

	SHIP DIRECT	DISTRIBUTION NETWORK	MIXED MODEL
DISTINGUISHING CHARACTERISTICS	Orders received directly from the end customer	Orders are received from another distributor that consolidate requirements from other distribution centers or retailers	Some products are shipped directly to end customers while others go through consolidators
MAJOR MANAGEMENT CONCERNS	Cost of shipping one at a time	Channel management Total cost of distribution and logistics Visibility of end customer demands	Channel management Total cost of distribution and logistics Visibility of end customer demands
TRADITIONAL STRATEGY	Orders are shipped directly to the customer	Minimum order quantities are set for the distributor	Minimum order quantities are set for the distributor
SOURCES OF PROBLEMS	Cost of communicating directly with each customer	Pricing and competitive factors between distribution networks	Pricing and competitive factors between distribution networks

Enterprise Requirements Summary

The table below summarizes the market-static enterprise characteristics. This information will be used in the next steps to prepare the internal and external supply-chain profiles.

Figure 5.5 **Static Characteristic Attribute Table—Enterprise Requirements Summary**

	SERVICE INDUSTRY	ENGINEERED PRODUCTS	PROCESS INDUSTRY	DISCRETE PRODUCTION	MIXED MODEL
DEMAND PROFILE	Repetitive Orders	Unique Orders	Seasonal Cycle	Product Cycle	Industry Cycle
FULFILLMENT APPROACH	Engineer-to-Order (ETO)	Make-to-Order (MTO)	Assemble-to-Order (ATO)	Build-to-Replenish (BTR)	Build-to-Forecast (BTF)
DISTRIBUTION		Ship Direct	Distribution Network	Mixed Model	

External Supply Chain

A company may be possibly engaged in multiple external supply chains based on the specific nature of the product line.

Figure 5.6 **External Supply Chain Profile**

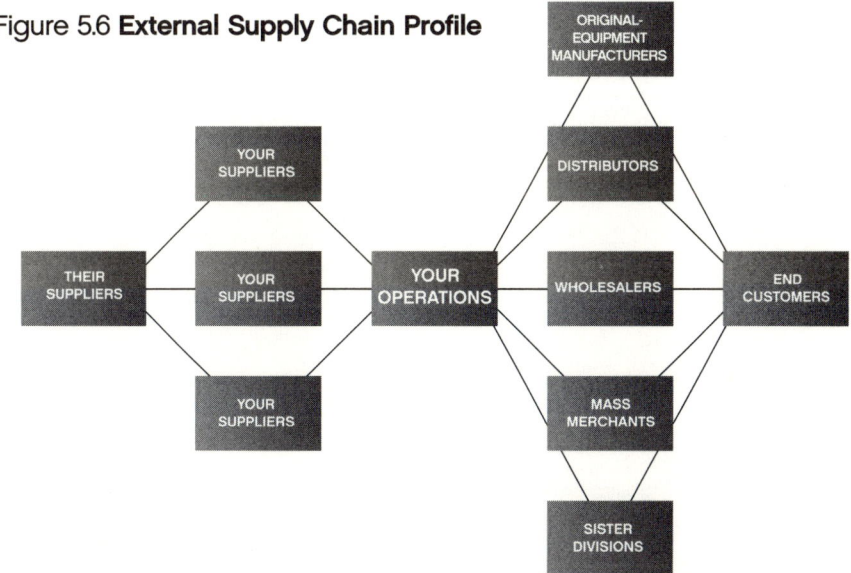

The external supply chain provides the visibility of the ecosystem surrounding the manufacturing company. The first step is to construct the high level product, cash, and information flows. This provides excellent insight into the linkages that have strong influences on the company. When constructing this profile, do not forget to highlight those enterprises in the chain that are also a part of your parent company. These sister companies can have a very strong influence on your performance—positive or negative.

Once the structure is completely built, the next step is to consider where the power and influence resides. While looking at your supply chain identify which link is the most influential or most powerful. This is commonly referred to as the 800 pound gorilla. The position of the 800 pound gorilla has a significant impact on the strategy that will be developed in the Improvement Phase.

Internal Supply Chain

The internal supply chain diagram provides a drill down into your manufacturing company. Take your company box and at a high level define the various functions that need to operate together to be successful. As you continue through the Theory

Figure 5.7 **Internal Supply Chain Profile**

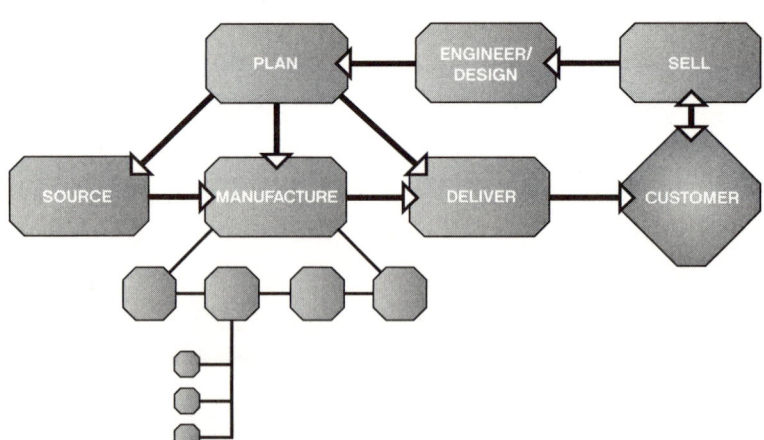

H.O.W. approach, you may find that the real improvement area may not be in the production area. The biggest opportunity is many times in a support function so do not overlook this step.

Product Flow Profile

The next step in the Theory H.O.W. approach is to drill down on the manufacturer process illustrated in the internal supply-chain profile above to understand the flow characteristics described by your product flow profile. The five possible choices are V.A.I.T. or combination of them. A "V" plant makes many different end items from relatively few raw materials. When the bills of material are examined for this type of company, they look

Figure 5.8 **V Plant**

Figure 5.9
A Plant

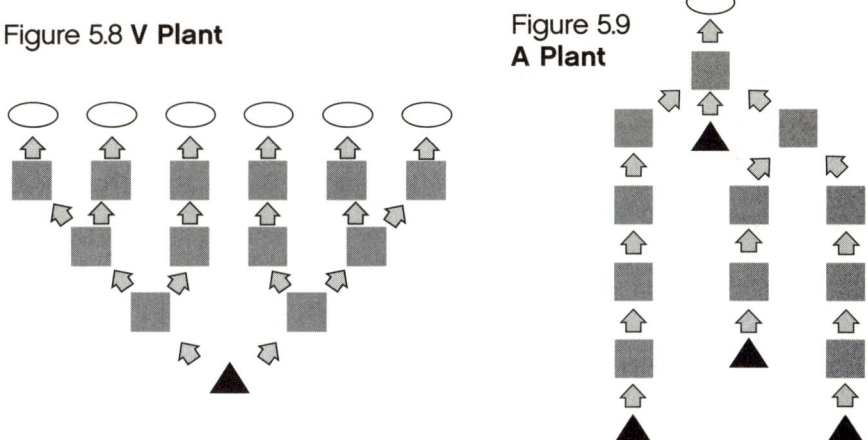

like a V. A "V" plant is usually make-to-stock and some of them are finish-to-order. On one hand "V" plants maintain a large variety of end items, and thus it might be difficult to maintain finished goods stock on all possible end items. However, consumer goods manufacturers are typically "V" plants. They may produce slow moving products as finish-to-order but maintain finished good inventories for all fast moving products.

Conversely, the "A" plant takes relatively many materials and produces fewer end items. "A" plants can easily embrace a make-to-order strategy. Building machines is a typical A structure and these are normally built to order. Smaller manufacturers are typically A plants, and they try to refrain from investing in finished goods stock due to the criticality of cash flow.

The "I' plant is a straight ahead assembly plant with a flowing assembly line. Think of a car assembly plant when thinking of an

"I" plant. In this kind of facility there is a continuous flow from the beginning to the end of the process.

A "T" plant postpones the final configuration of the end item until the very last possible moment. "T" plants are most commonly an assemble-to-order strategy.

Figure 5.10 **I Plant**   Figure 5.11 **T Plant**

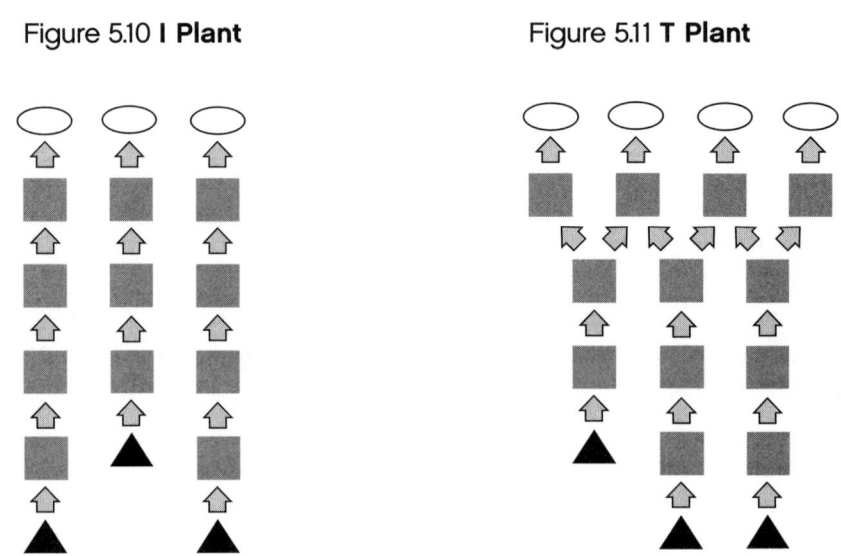

Figure 5.12 **Combination/Mixed Model Plant**

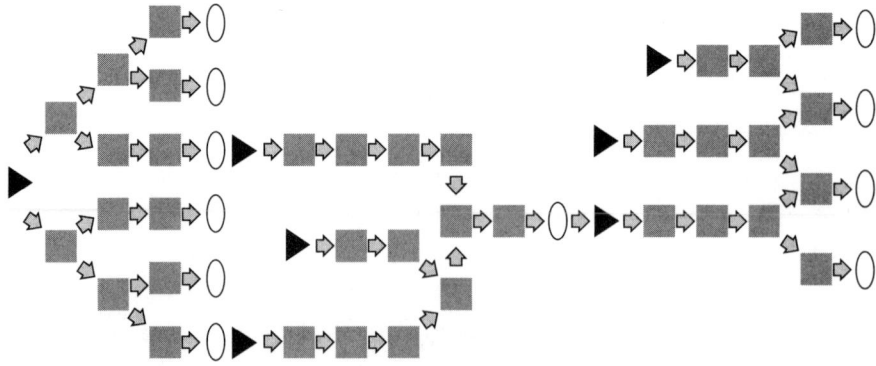

Figure 5.13 **Product Flow Analysis and Evaluation**

	V-PLANT	A-PLANT	I-PLANT	T-PLANT	MIXED MODEL
DISTINGUISHING CHARACTERISTICS	Number of end items is large compared to the number of raw materials All end items sold are produced in essentially the same process Equipment is generally capital intensive and highly specialized	Assembly of large number of parts into a relatively small number of end items Components are unique to a specific end item Routings are dissimilar Machines and tooling are general purpose	Assembly on a capital intensive assembly line Many different configurations are possible Routings are identical Machines and tooling are specialized	Assembly of common parts into the final product Components common to many end items Routings dissimilar Routings may or may not include divert or assembly processes	The process is a combination of several types of plants. For example, a V plant may feed an A plant or an I plant could feed a V plant.
MAJOR MANAGEMENT CONCERNS	Finished goods inventories are too high Customer service is poor Manufacturing cites apparent constant change in demand Marketing cites lack of responsiveness from manufacturing Interdepartmental conflicts are common within the manufacturing operations	Chronic assembly shortages Excess unplanned overtime Resource utilization (not activation) is unsatisfactory Production bottlenecks seem to wander from resource to resource Operation appears out of control and in constant fire fighting mode	Synchronizing the incoming raw material to arrive in sequence to meet the line If the line goes down there is no recovery Workers become specialists in one area but may become bored	Large finished goods and component inventories Poor delivery performance: (40% early, 20% on time, 40% late) Excessive fabrication time Unsatisfactory resource utilization in fabrication Fabrication and assembly treated as separate plants	Concerns are relative to the combination involved
TRADITIONAL STRATEGY	Improve customer service by: increasing finished goods inventory and improving forecasting capabilities Reduce production costs by: reducing direct labor content reducing scrap improving yields	Focus on the improvement of the efficiency at each stage of the operation Control the use of overtime Focus engineering efforts on reducing unit cost of production to offset inefficiencies	Change the line over once per year in response to model changes Keep the line running and all the equipment available	Improve deliveries off the shelf by developing better product forecasting techniques and improving inventory and planning functions Reduce the product cost by improving efficiencies Reduce cost through "optimal" product design and product proliferation Reduce labor cost through automation and new technology	Depends on the specific combination
SOURCE OF PROBLEMS	Excess capacity Common material usage leading to material misallocation	Shared resources Resource misallocation	Little flexibility on the line outside the defined configurations and rates	Common material usage Material misallocation	Manage complex combinations

Inventory Profile

Inventory is an excellent identifier for the effectiveness of the process and to identify where opportunity areas exist. The next step in the Theory H.O.W. approach is to use the external and internal supply-chain diagrams developed previously in this chapter and identify where the pools of inventory exist.

Figure 5.14 **Internal Inventory Profile**

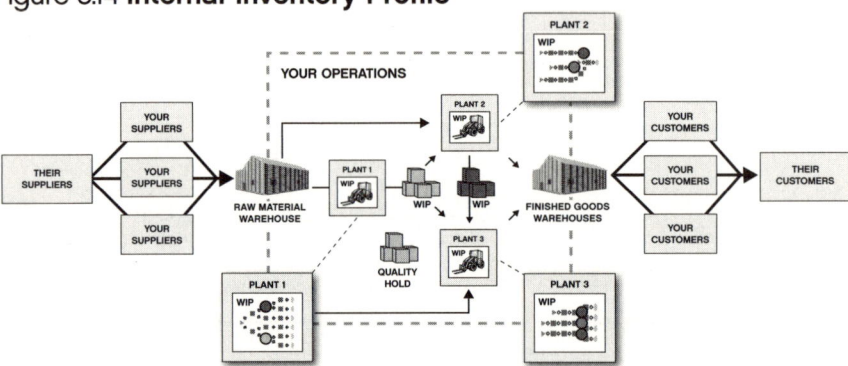

Inventory will pool in front of a physical constraints or in response to uncertainty or unreliability of the process. Ensure that all inventory is accounted for—raw material, work in process, on hold, finished goods, in transit, etc. Mapping the amount of inventory in the internal and external supply chains is similar to the doctor taking your blood pressure and temperature. That does not provide a diagnosis but if the readings are

Figure 5.15 **External Inventory Profile**

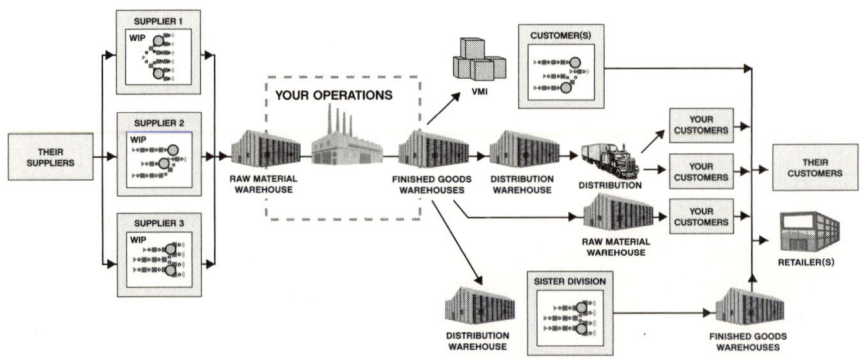

off the expected values, it does provide information on where to look. Remember to consider not only your own inventory but also the inventory of your suppliers and customers. Nobody in the supply makes any profit until the end customer buys. Simply looking internal to your own company will not reveal the best answer.

Developing Your Company Performance Profile

The last step in the learning phase is to understand your company's performance on a set of critical measures. We call these measures the Crazy Eight. You would be crazy to not measure these eight critical measures. Not only is the specific number important but the performance over time provides even more insight into the process.

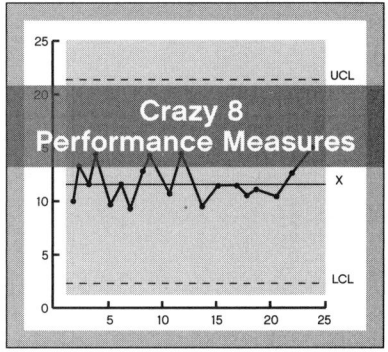

1. **Delivery Performance:** There are three dimensions to delivery performance. First is a summary of the performance to request and the performance to promise. Many companies set a goal for delivery to promise and totally miss the valuable market insight understanding the customer's true desires. The delivery to promise can be

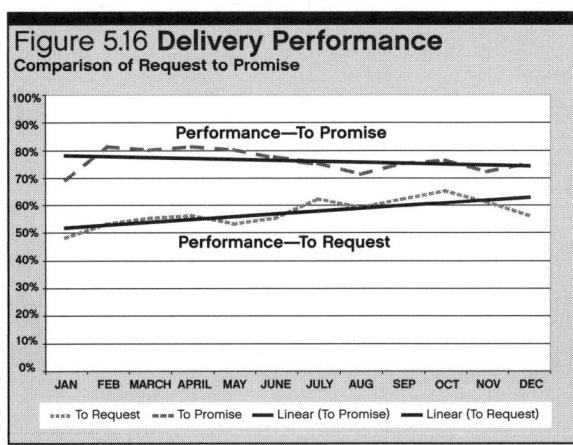

100% only to discover that the customer's needs are not being met. The second dimension is detail around the performance to promise. Look at the variability of timeliness. A supplier that is consistent

but late is far better than a supplier that is sometimes early and sometimes late. The customer has to buffer with inventory for those times the supplier is late and store excess inventory when the supplier is early. Consistency is key. The third dimension is the detail around the performance to request. Again look at the consistency of the performance. This can be the source of a unique value proposition that will be developed during the Improvement Phase.

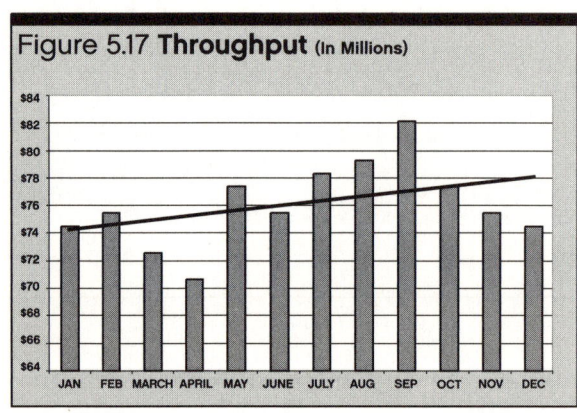

2. **Throughput (T):** Throughput is defined as the rate at which the system generates money through sales. It is calculated as sales - totally variable expense (s-tve). Totally variable expense (tve) are those items that if you didn't have the sale, you wouldn't have written the check.

3. **Investment (I):** Investment is all of the money the system spends on things it intends to turn into throughput but is still around. Common things considered investmentinclude raw materials (at the price paid to the vendor), work in process, finished goods, buildings, equipment, other assets, and know-how.

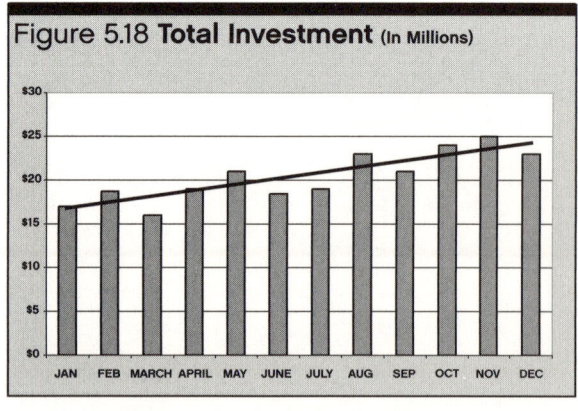

4. Operating Expense (OE): Operating expense is all of the money the system spends in order to turn inventory into throughput. Items included may be salaries, wages, benefits, utilities, insurance, lease, interest, taxes, etc. Operating expense is not just another term for "fixed costs".

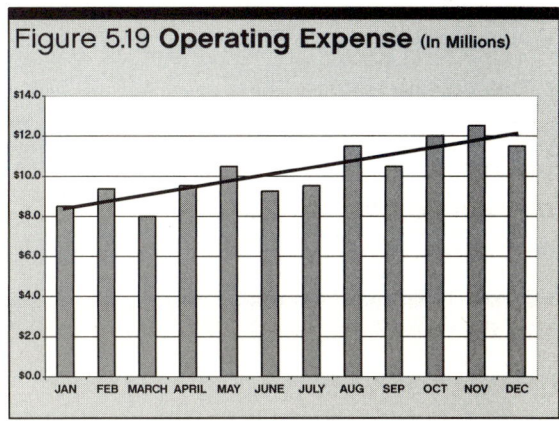

Figure 5.19 **Operating Expense** (In Millions)

5. Product Cost Breakdown: Understand the components of the product cost. What is the percentage of material, labor, and overhead allocation in the product? Is there a specific component of overhead that dominates that category? Many consumer goods companies spend much more on product promotion than they do on direct labor. Transportation costs may even be buried in the overhead number. With recent moves to outsource production overseas, it is important to understand where those costs are hiding.

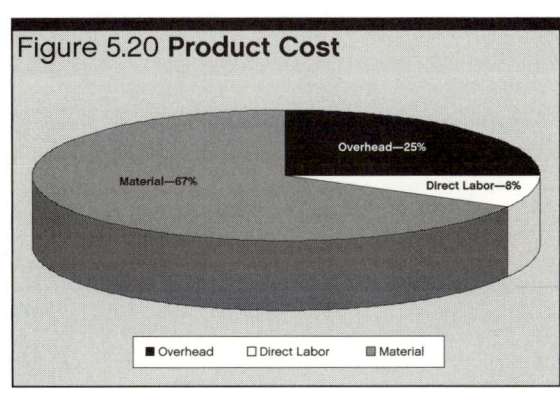

Figure 5.20 **Product Cost**

6. **T/I Ratio:**
This ratio is
throughput
divided by invest-
ment. This is an
alternate way to
calculate inven-
tory turns. This
calculation takes
out the account-
ing value earned

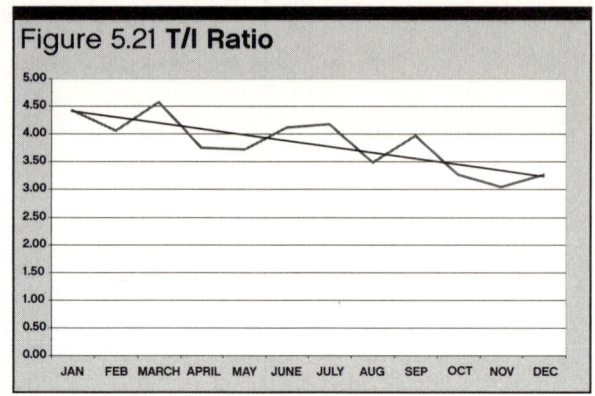

Figure 5.21 **T/I Ratio**

when inventory is built in excess of requirements.

7. **T/OE Ratio:** This ratio is throughput divided by operating

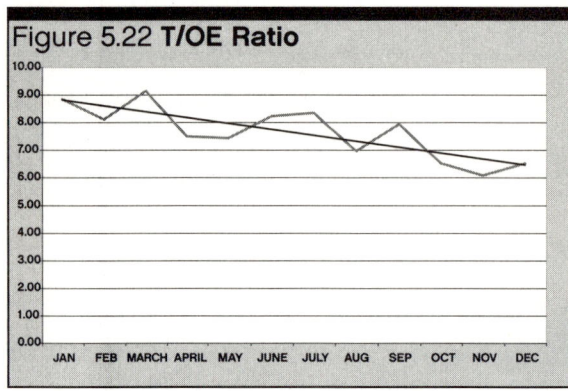

Figure 5.22 **T/OE Ratio**

expense. This pro-
ductivity measure
when graphed over
time provides ex-
cellent insight into
overall system per-
formance. Do you
see a repeating pat-
tern?

8. **Manufacturing Lead
Time:** Lead time is
defined as the elapsed
time from the release of
a manufacturing authori-
zation until the receipt of
the finished product
ready to go to the cus-
tomer. Different parts
will likely have different

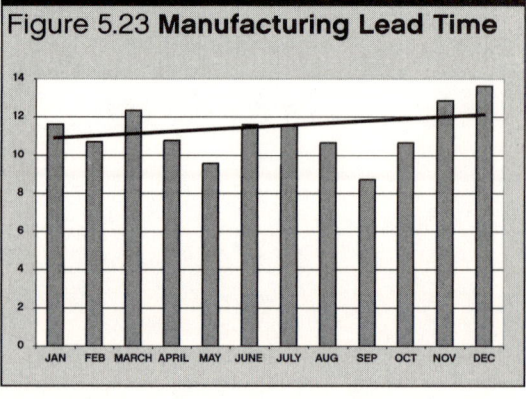

Figure 5.23 **Manufacturing Lead Time**

lead times; however parts can be collected into product families to develop this graph.

On all these charts use SPC (statistical process control) tools to evaluate the performance over time. Is the performance metric in statistical control with little variability? Is there a trend over time? Do you see a repeating pattern? All of these patterns provide tremendous insight into the overall company performance. If you do not have a background in SPC, find a Six Sigma professional or refer to the appendix for references in this area. SPC will provide you with significant insight into your processes as you look at the key measures over time.

Summary

The learning phase provides a rich insight into the current reality of your company. The next phase is the diagnostic phase where this critical business information will be gleaned for the vital few items that can make a breakthrough difference for your company.

Figure 5.24 **Business Rules Zone Summary—Who You Are: SEC**

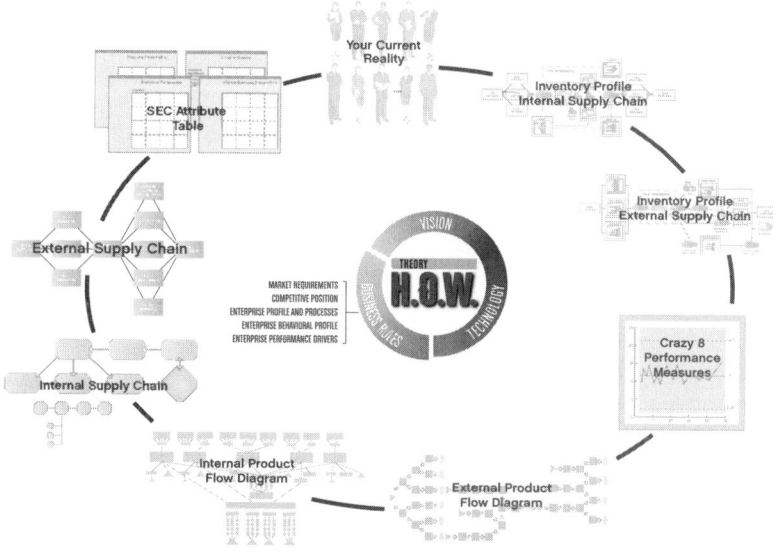

References

Synchronous Management, Umble, Srikanth

Chapter 6
Diagnostic Phase Dynamic Enterprise Characteristics

Introduction

As described in Chapter 5, in the short term a company cannot change inherent characteristics that define its culture, approach to the market, and competitive position. These are defined as static enterprise characteristics. However, a company can make dramatic operational improvements. Monitoring and addressing the appropriate dynamic enterprise characteristics provides the company with a realtime competitive position in its marketplace. This chapter will explore those dynamic enterprise characteristics and begin the process of determining the best strategic objective to drive significant results.

DEC (Dynamic Enterprise Characteristics)—Definition

DEC (dynamic enterprise characteristics) are specific conditions that are the results of the current operating parameters. Executives control these attributes through strategic programs and improvement processes. These conditions can and will change as the organization modifies its mode of operation in response to changes in market conditions. In addition, dynamic enterprise characteristics will change as the company implements specific improvements. Dynamic enterprise characteristics are driven by the overall vision and form the basis for the organization's improvement strategy.

Diagnostic Phase Objective

In this diagnostic phase, information is pulled from the profile completed in Chapter 4, The Theory H.O.W. Approach and Chapter 5, Static Enterprise Characteristics. This part of the Theory H.O.W. approach begins the process of gleaning the vital few focus items from amidst the useful many items identified. From these data a diagnosis can be made about the next logical move for the company. Once that goal has been achieved then your company can evaluate its next move based on the dynamic enterprise characteristics once again. The Theory H.O.W. approach has been developed to provide a repeatable ongoing improvement process for a company.

The objective of this phase is to accelerate the improvement cycle in order to achieve incremental and breakthrough benefits. In addition, an overall attitude is created in the company to challenge the status quo. Inertia must not be allowed to settle into the organization.

Figure 6.1 **Incremental Improvement**

Figure 6.2 **Breakthrough Improvement**

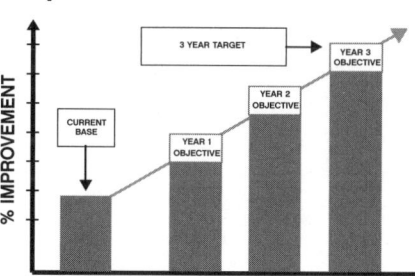

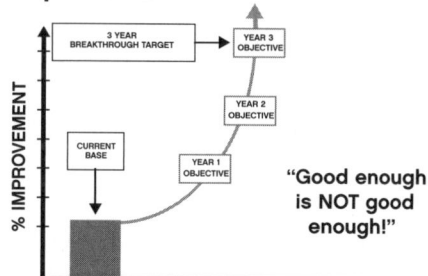

As seen in the graph, incremental improvement, while still improvement, falls far short of the breakthrough improvement potential. As we discussed in Chapter 4, the idea of Archimedes on Fire is that by iteratively addressing the constraints limiting the organization's ability to achieve its desired goal, dramatic improvements can be made to the bottomline.

Figure 6.3 **Best Practices Cloud**

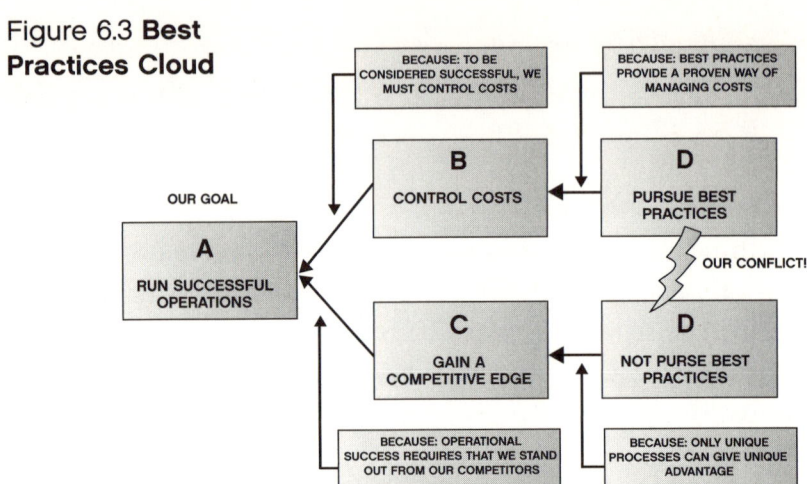

In order to run a successful operation, every manager struggles with the conflict inherent in pursuing best practices. According to an excellent analysis performed by Bob Reary as he struggled with this in his own position, every manager needs to control costs to be considered successful. In order to control costs, the path of least resistance is to pursue industry best practices. This is encouraged by many software and consulting companies to speed technological implementations. However, at the same time to gain a competitive advantage a company must stand out from its competitors. To stand out from its competitors, unique processes are required. To help you through this process, in this phase of the approach you will:

▶ Review the organized data collected in previous chapters.

▶ Separate what's interesting from what's relevant.

▶ Begin to turn data into information and intelligence.

▶ Isolate the cause/effect relationships that are affecting the enterprise and determine what is limiting it from achieving its goals.

▶ Begin to formulate strategies that will be supported by specific tactical actions through the process described in Chapter 7 to achieve your desired goal.

Vision Development

In Chapter 4 the elements of an effective vision were discussed. The vision for your company comes from the uniqueness of your company. Also, your company has to provide value to its customers at a profit to itself. This vision provides the driver and the context for everything else your company does. The vision forms the framework for the mandate to change. How many times have you heard "I'll know it when I see it" as the answer to the question "What are you looking for?" Your company cannot achieve its full potential with that level of confusion. Think about the static enterprise characteristics you developed for your company in Chapter 5. Are you the 800 pound Gorilla in the supply chain or are you the canary? What is your importance to the supply chain? Is your product a commodity where you compete mostly on price, or do you make a custom product for which you are the only source in the world? How about lead time? Is there value to your customer to have a short lead time? The only sustainable competitive advantage is when you can solve your customer's business problem at a profit to yourself.

Get into your customer's head. What is its number one issue or the constraint to achieving its goal? How can you help with that? Is due date performance critical? If you try to convince yourself that all your customer cares about is price, then you do not truly understand your customer. Do not be lazy and stop at the easy answer of price. The real answer is not price. Remember that all your customer cares about is its business and improving its overall profitability. One way to do that is to have lower prices from suppliers—you. Lowering price is a win-lose value proposition. The customer wins and you lose. This is not a sustainable vision.

1. Spend time with a representative sample of your customers.

2. Understand what their constraint is to increased profitability.

3. How can your company address this?

This part of the process is for you to think about your competitive position, and not consider only price.

After considering all these questions, what is that "one thing," that uniqueness that your company has, that provides value to your customer at a profit to yourself? Your vision should be expressed in one sentence. This should set you apart from your competition and be something that they cannot easily copy.

It should not be a meaningless statement like, "We will be the premier provider of product X at a profit to ourselves, provide a great place to work, and we will be kind to the environment." It should be something like, "We will shrink our leadtimes so much shorter than our customer's demand cycle that no change they make can possibly hurt us."

To further validate that your vision is relevant, consider the following competitive element matrix. This matrix does not need to have exact precision. Do not spend hundreds of hours collecting data. This is the time for "good enough."

Getting the idea of where you stand is certainly more important than getting the fourth digit past the decimal point accurate.

Figure 6.4 **Competitive Element Matrix**

	WEIGHT	MARKET REQUIREMENTS	YOUR PERFORMANCE	YOUR COMPETITORS	YOUR RANK
PRODUCT	20%	Good enough	Great	Fair	▲
PRICE	10%	Cheap	Fair	Great	▼
DELIVERY PERFORMANCE	20%	Excellent	Good	Poor	▲
LEAD TIME	30%	Fair	Poor	Fair	▼
QUALITY	10%	Excellent	Fair	Excellent	▼
SERVICE	10%	Good	Excellent	Good	▲
OVERALL					◄ ►

The goal of this exercise is to get an idea of what is important to the customer, how does your company rate, and how does your competitor rate.

Remember the story of the two hikers in the woods. They came upon a bear and started to run for their lives. One stopped and began to unlace his boots and put on tennis shoes. The other scoffed and said that he would never outrun the bear just because he changed his shoes. That hiker reminded the other that he did not need to outrun the bear—just the other hiker.

And so it goes with competition. It does not matter how far in front you are of your competition. In fact, it is better to just stay a bit ahead. If you get too far ahead you may be giving away your future competitive advantage. Better to hold something back and when your competition catches up just hit the booster rocket and speed out in front once again. It is far better to have something in reserve than to be completely stretched out all the time.

Not every competitive element has the same weight from the customer's perspective. This depends on the industry you defined in the static enterprise characteristics. Lead time may be critical and price secondary if your company is heavily engineer to order. A combination of variety and lead time is important if you assemble to order.

Critically look at each element and assess a relative weight to it. One suggestion that has been effective many times over is to take 100% and divide it across each element in its relative weight. This provides the necessary perspective for the comparison of the elements for your company and a way to bring focus to those items that really matter to your company.

Keep in mind that this is not a static one-time effort. Market condition and competitive performance change on a regular basis affecting the way your company typically functions. Even though you have changed into your sneakers, never take your eyes off the others in the race. They may be closer than they they truly appear.

Figure 6.5 **Critical Success Factors by Industry Type**

SERVICE INDUSTRY	ENGINEERED PRODUCTS	HEAVY PROCESS	DISCRETE PRODUCTION	MIXED MODEL
Wait time	Design quality	Product variety	Lead time	Combination of different types (discrete, process, engineered, service)
Customer experience	Lead time	Cost	Product variety	

In the table above, the static enterprise characteristic attribute table for industry is revisited. For each of the possible industries the most typical critical competitive elements have been defined. This is not to say that the competitive elements may be different in your company. The table is provided to suggest a starting place to look.

What Is the Goal?

What would seem to be a simple question to answer is actually quite difficult. Everyone who read *The Goal* would quickly answer "to make money now and into the future." This is indeed true. However, at this point you need to be more specific.

In Chapter 5 you identified what your company was in terms of its static enterprise characteristics as summarized in the table below. In addition, you mapped in an SPC format the company's performance against the crazy eight key measurements.

Figure 6.6 **Static Characteristic Attribute Table Summary**

INDUSTRY TYPE	Service industry	Engineered Products	Process Industry	Discrete Production	Mixed Model
DEMAND PROFILE	Repetitive	Unique	Seasonal Cycle	Product Cycle	Industry Cycle
FULFILLMENT APPROACH	Engineer-To-Order (ETO)	Make-To-Order (MTO)	Assemble-To-Order (ATO)	Build-To-Replenish (BTR)	Build-To-Forecast (BTF)
DISTRIBUTION		Ship Direct	Distribution Network	Mixed Model	
OPERATIONAL STRUCTURE	V	A	I	T	Combination

In this chapter so far you have begun to develop your vision—that unique thing that you can provide the customer at a profit to yourself. These two items are linked together by the goal and the goal validates each of these.

Your Profile	Your GOAL	Your Vision
Who You Are? (SEC)	What Is Your GOAL?	Who Do You Want to Be?

Constraints to the Goal

Remember the constraints discussion in Chapter 2 in the Preparation phase. These constraints set the framework for the limitations that you may encounter as you pursue your goal. Consider each of these questions as you think about your vision and desired goal.

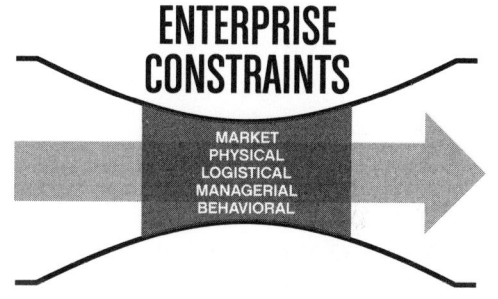

Market—Is your value proposition compelling to the market? If you can produce more than what the market is demanding then your constraint is in the market. This is the time to create a compelling value proposition. They are more fully described in Chapter 7. Having a compelling value proposition can allow you to exploit that excess capacity and dramatically improve profitability since you are able to significantly increase throughput with a very little increase in operating expense.

Physical—Assess your product and process quality. Are you fully exploiting your process constraints? Is it really running all the time on the correct mix and sequence of products? Are you using statistical process control techniques or are you still attempting to inspect quality into the product manufactured? What is your current state of technology? Does your technology add value or does it get in the way of what people really need to be doing?

Logistical—What is your fulfillment process? Does this process run smoothly or does it require extensive hand holding. How accurate is your forecasting process? Do you collaborate with your customers and partners to develop the forecast? How dependable is your logistical system? Can you reliably get parts from all your vendors? A constraint for many companies is raw material itself. If the availability of raw material is insufficient to make everything you have orders for—then material is your constraint. Selecting which products to build that maximize your throughput per unit of constraint material becomes a critical dynamic enterprise characteristic.

Managerial—Look at the other departments in the internal supply chain that you developed in Chapter 5. Is your constraint in one of those departments and not on the production floor? This is determined the same way as a physical constraint is determined. Where is the work piled up? This does not need to be an ultra sophisticated process. Simply by asking the question where things get "stuck" you can quickly determine where the managerial bottleneck resides. The order entry process or engineering processes are frequently the real constraints to achieving your vision rather than the production process.

Consider also the performance measurements for procurement. Does this department earn incentives by purchasing the cheapest part or the parts that enable your company to be the most profitable? What is the treatment of suppliers? Is there a win-win collaborative approach or does the purchasing department simply beat them for price?

A key managerial constraint for every company is cash. Cash is king, especially in smaller companies. Frequently a company will trade profitability for improved cash flow. When you have no cash, it is irrelevant how profitable you are since you can't pay your bills. Do not be surprised to see cash as a critical constraint that must be exploited.

Behavioral—Behavior can only be modified through education and reinforcement of the desired behavior. Do the executives expect excellence or is shoddy workmanship acceptable? Do the rules change depending on how badly the revenue is needed? How well are the business systems utilized in the company? Is the software just running on the computer or is it really a mission critical system? How are the people in the organization rewarded? Is it consistent with your desired goal? If behavior does not match expectations, check the measures. People are generally a very predictable animal. They will behave consistently with how they are measured. If you don't like the behavior—change the measures.

Performance Measures Evaluation

At the end of Chapter 5, the "crazy eight" performance measures were introduced and the suggestion made to graph these over time. These measures were:

1. Delivery performance—performance to request and performance to promise.

2. Throughput (T)

3. Investment (I)

4. Operating expense (OE)

5. Product cost breakdown

6. T/I Ratio (Inventory turns)

7. T/OE Ratio (Productivity)

8. Manufacturing lead time

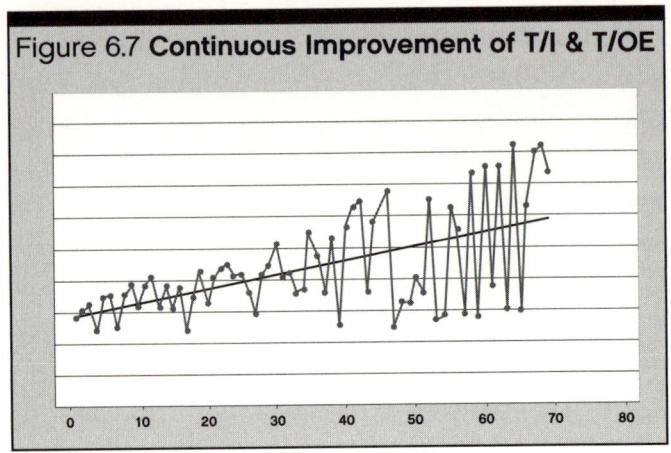

Figure 6.7 **Continuous Improvement of T/I & T/OE**

When you look at these graphs, do you see a pattern occuring over time?

This figure shows what continuous improvement looks like from beginning to end. This is a desirable graph for throughput, T/I, and the T/OE. This would be very undesirable as a graph for all the other measures since it would show continuous deterioration of the process. Even though the overall trend is somewhat improving, the consistency of the measure is not doing the same.

True continuous improvement will improve not only the measure over time, but also the overall consistency of that improved performance.

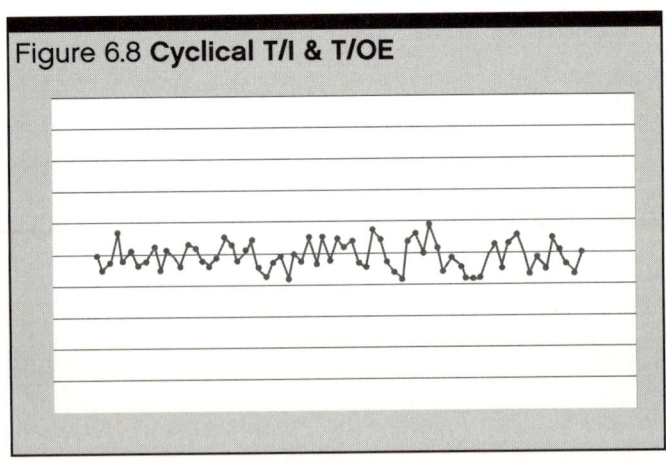

Figure 6.8 **Cyclical T/I & T/OE**

This figure shows a cyclical pattern on a monthly basis. This is a very common pattern in a discrete manufacturing company. However, this is also very bad. This figure shows a significant nonlinearity in the overall process, but the consistency is far better than the previous chart.

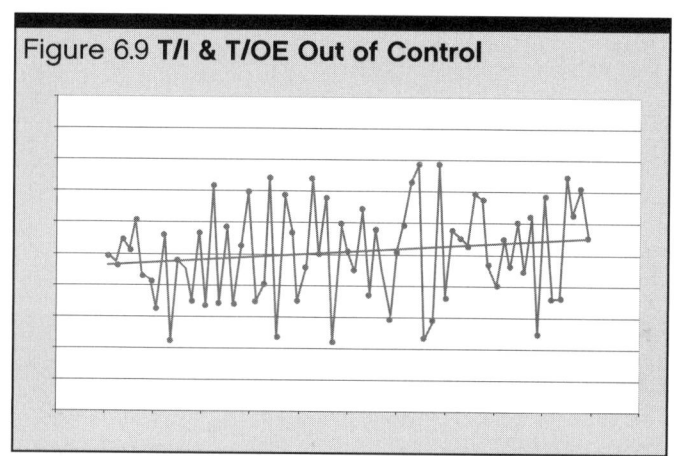

Figure 6.9 **T/I & T/OE Out of Control**

These results are highly variable and shows a company that is out of control. The first step for this company would be to gain control of the process and improve consistency. The next step here would be operational improvement.

What other patterns do you see in your charts? This is an excellent opportunity to bring in your Six Sigma professionals with their extensive statistical analysis toolbox to help you discover inherent information on the overall process.

Strategic Challenges and Opportunities

The next step is to explore strategic challenges and strategic opportunities that may arise. These opportunities are covered in the same section because so many times they are the opposite sides of the same coin. Determining which depends on the response from the entire management team.

In the Chinese language, the word for crisis is comprised of two different symbols—one for danger and the other one for opportunity.

Figure 6.10 **Determining Your Strategic Challenges and Opportunities**

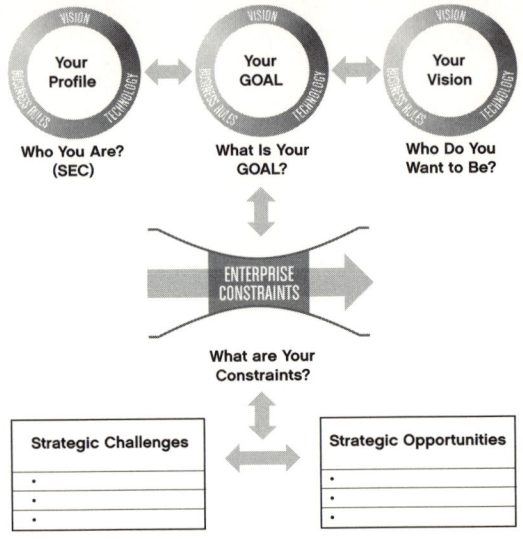

**What Are Your Strategic
Challenges and Opportunities?**

The hyper-competitive world for manufacturers today is teeming with dangerous opportunities.

In the Learning Phase you developed an internal supply chain diagram and an external supply chain diagram. Now look at that diagram and determine where the influencer is in that supply chain.

Do not confuse size for influence. Just because a company or enterprise is large does not necessarily mean they are the gorilla in the supply chain. Very small companies can control a significant position of power with the right strategy.

We refer to the company with the greatest influence and power as the gorilla. The other companies in the supply chain are the canaries.

If you are the canary feeding the gorilla, how can you gain the gorilla's attention and become a valued supplier?

The key is to become an integral part of their organization and so sticky that the organiziation would never even consider replacing you.

Figure 6.11 **Supply Chain Influence** Position 1

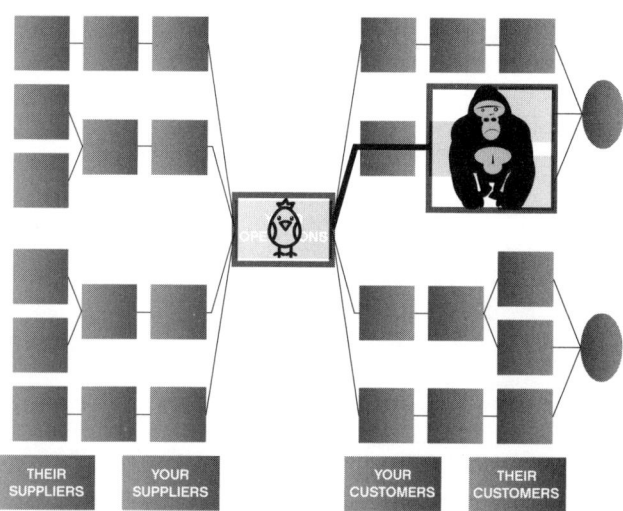

Is the gorilla prior to you in the supply chain? How can you assure yourself of sufficient materials at a reasonable price? What value can you bring to their organization? This is a more difficult position to be in than being the supplier to the gorilla.

Figure 6.12 **Supply Chain Influence** Position 2

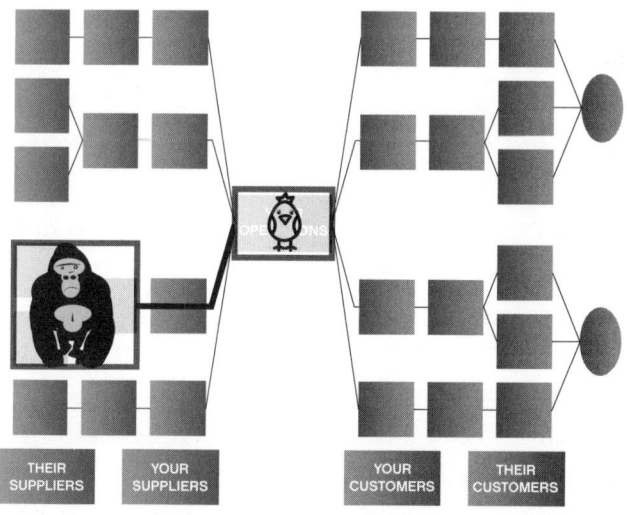

You may find that you are at the mercy of this dominant force. Your next step would be to collaborate with your down-

Figure 6.13 **Supply Chain Influence** Position 3

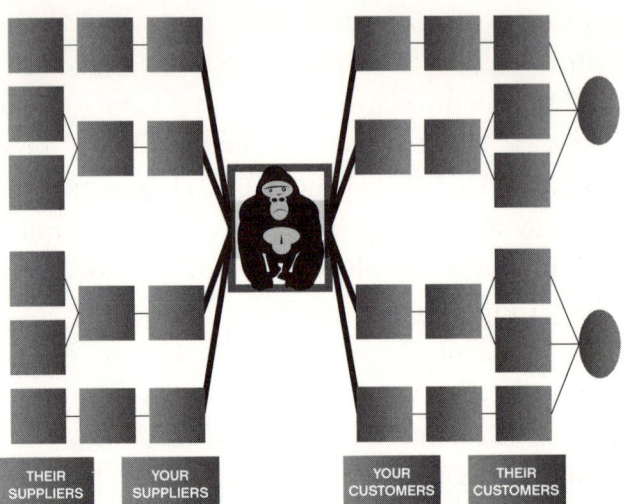

| THEIR SUPPLIERS | YOUR SUPPLIERS | YOUR CUSTOMERS | THEIR CUSTOMERS |

stream customers to mitigate the impact of the gorilla. Finally, what if you are the gorilla? How can you help your strategic suppliers to be more reliable and help you improve your operations? By working together to create a win-win, a sustainable competitive advantage is achieved. This is an excellent place to be. You have the opportunity to positively impact not only your suppliers but also your customers.

As you consider the outside influences, is there a challenge facing you that you can turn into an opportunity? So many times companies look at things that are generally perceived to be negatives as a burden that must be overcome. These truly are dangerous opportunities. Instead, look for the silver lining in that cloud. How can you turn that negative into a positive by leading the way for the industry?

Dynamic Enterprise Characteristic Development

The final step in the diagnostic phase is to list the DEC (dynamic enterprise characteristics) that are the vital few necessary to manage the company. These are absolutely unique by each company and will likely change over time as the process is improved. The DECs are a combination of key performance attributes that are monitored to determine the overall progress of the company, an awareness of external enterprise conditions in the market place, and a measure of competitor effectiveness. Think about the vision and the goal you defined in this chapter. How do you know you have achieved it? The dynamic enterprise characteristics should number no more than 3-5 key indicators. Keep it simple. A break-through strategy is one that improves all the dynamic enterprise characteristics simultaneously. This is not a balanced scorecard with all its complexity and conflict. The entire DEC process is about finding the Archimedes on Fire leverage point, not finding an optimization point. Attempting to optimize one measure against another one only leads to both falling short of expectation. If you find yourself with measures that seemingly conflict or you are forced to optimize, then you have not uncovered the break-through improvement idea yet.

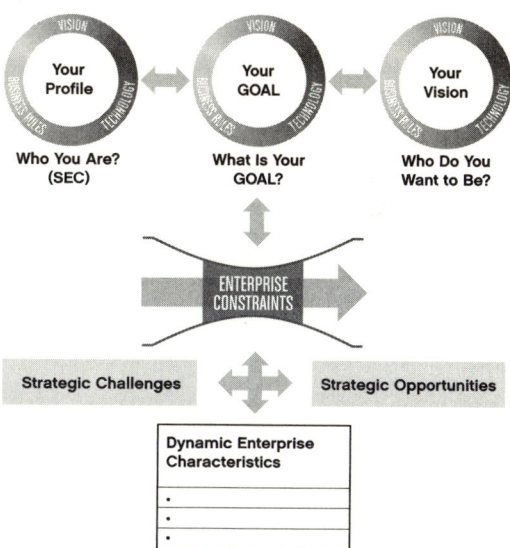

Figure 6.14 **What Are the DEC that are going to drive your breakthrough improvement process?**

There are three dimensions to the dynamic enterprise characteristic. First consider the driving force or relevance behind the DEC. Did the DEC come from being a canary between two gorillas or from ineffectively managing a T-type process? The second dimension is the impact on the current reality. The DEC should bring focus to the leverage point. Last, what is the magnitude of the opportunity if the DEC is addressed and improved? Remember, you are looking for the leverage point and the results will be significant not marginal. The DEC always align with the vision and goal. Refer to the complementary workbook, *Theory H.O.W. To* for several examples of this completed process.

Summary

In this chapter, the dynamic enterprise characteristics were developed by identifying the vision, the goal, and the strategic challenges and opportunities. The overall vision exploits what is unique to your company that creates value for your customer at a profit to your company. The goal identifies a desired measurable future state. The DECs are those few items (3-5) that bring focus to the journey to the goal. There will be many goals on the trip towards the vision. Strategic challenges will be faced that will pull you away from your goal. At the same time, strategic opportunities will present themselves that help push you towards your goal. Effectively understanding and managing these two opposing forces is critical to your overall success. The diagnostic phase is all about determining what is significant and vital out of the teeming mass of what is interesting. Just as a doctor considers many symptoms before making a diagnosis, you have considered significant information before putting your finger on Archimedes' leverage point. Now you are prepared to move into the Improvement phase where specific strategic objectives will be identified and detailed.

Figure 6.15 **Vision Zone Summary – What Is the Goal and DEC?**

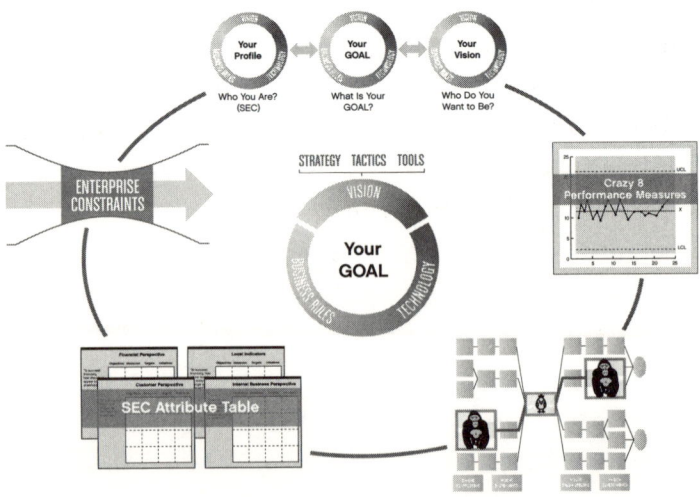

Chapter 7
Defining an Improvement Solution

Introduction

Now that you have developed an understanding of the static enterprise characteristics in Chapter 5 and the dynamic enterprise characteristics in Chapter 6, the next step is to select the strategic objectives and breakthrough improvement projects. These objectives could be an operational improvement or strategic improvement solution. The operational improvement solutions enable you to improve performance such that you are ready for a strategic improvement. If your DEC evaluation is over the necessary threshold then you may be able to go directly to the strategic improvement solution. The matrix on the next page begins the process of defining your next step.

Figure 7.1 *Theory H.O.W.* Next Step Recommendation Matrix

STATIC ENTERPRISE CHARACTERISTIC ATTRIBUTE SUMMARY TABLE

INDUSTRY TYPE	Service Industry 111, 129	Engineered Products 103, 109, 110, 126	Process Industry 106, 112, 129	Discrete Production 103, 117, 121, 129	Mixed Model 103, 106, 117, 129
DEMAND PROFILE	Repetitive 106, 113, 117, 121	Unique 103, 110, 117, 126	Seasonal Cycle 103, 112	Product Cycle 106, 113	Industry Cycle 103, 112
FULFILLMENT APPROACH	ETO 103, 109, 110, 111, 126	MTO 103, 109, 121	ATO 103, 109, 117, 121	BTR 106, 112, 114, 117	BTF 112, 113, 114, 117
DISTRIBUTION	Ship Direct 103, 111, 113, 114	Distribution Network 106, 113, 114, 121	Mixed Model 109, 114, 121		
OPERATIONAL STRUCTURE	V 103, 110, 126	A 106, 114, 117	I 106, 129	T 103, 109	Combination 103, 117, 129

This table summarizes key static enterprise characteristics. Under each entry, there are page numbers that recommend a possible solution for your company. The top row of numbers in each box is the possible strategic improvement solution that may fit your company. The bottom row of number is the operational improvement solution. Keep a list of the numbers that are below the characteristic that you circled in Chapter 5. Tally how many times each number comes up. If your firm has alignment in its process, one of the solution numbers will stand out. Provided that there is good alignment, the Pareto principle will hold true. As you compare suggestions from each row, the number of times a possible solution comes up will provide a relative weight for the solution. If you see a great divergence in the recommendations provided in the matrix, this means that you should go directly to the operational improvement solution areas. Remember that this matrix is a non-dynamic way to offer guidance based on your self assessment through the Theory H.O.W. approach. It is based on your team's ability to correctly evaluate and create your company's static enterprise characteristics and dynamic enterprise characteristics. To see an example that has been worked out for a real company, please refer to the complementary workbook, *Theory H.O.W. To.*

STRATEGIC IMPROVEMENT SOLUTIONS

Quick Response

The essence of this solution is that customers will be willing to pay for guaranteed deliveries that are faster than the competitors can deliver. If the customer frequently suffers from shortages that significantly impact their operation this solution may be a solution for you. This happens when the market lead time is relatively long (greater than 6 weeks) and the standard delivery performance by the industry is relatively poor (less than 80%). Check this in your competitive element matrix you prepared during the Diagnostic Phase in Chapter 6. The assumption here is that orders are typically built to forecast. Your manufacturing facility is currently either building to forecast or building to replenishment. The last thing to check is that the price of your product is fairly low as compared to the customer's selling price. You will likely find this most when you are the canary feeding the gorilla in the supply chain. When this happens, the damage of not having your product when it is needed is much greater than the cost of your product itself. Even though your customer may be asking you for lower price, what they really want is faster delivery on a more reliable basis. One caution is if your product is a commodity. If it is a commodity, the customer may find it easy to pursue an alternative solution. The Internet has made it so easy to just change suppliers quickly. This risk is mitigated if the customer does repeat business with you or if the number of parts you provide to them is relatively high. When the number of parts is high, then it is more costly for the customer to manage the increase in stock levels across the board rather than paying a premium for guaranteed expedited delivery. A good example of this type of environment is labels. A customer can use thousands of different labels. The cost of each is very small but their product cannot ship without the right label. The cost of being out is then very high. The customer cannot get online and easily purchase a label from another supplier since it is a custom product for them.

If you have frequent emergency orders from your customers, then you may be very successful with this solution. However, before you can pursue this solution your overall delivery performance must be very close to 100%. If your company cannot reliably perform to this level then your first step will be the operational improvement solution found on page 129.

If you do pursue this solution, sell the customer the idea of the win-win offer. The customer pays you a premium for guaranteed quicker deliveries. The guarantee is that you will pay a high penalty to them if you miss the delivery. This solution can be further segmented into super express service. For example, if the market lead time is six weeks and you can guarantee that you can deliver in two weeks, you will also have some customers who want delivery in three days. This is super express delivery and the customer will generally believe it is impossible. This delivery bears an even higher price premium (and penalty guarantee). You can expect that about one third of your volume will be the rapid service offer. About 10% of that will be the super express. This is important when you set up your reserve buffer capacity in your production plan. If you are not currently using buffer management in your production process, it is critical to implement buffer management before you attempt this. Otherwise you will fail miserably.

Surprisingly, this extra cost guarantee offer will bring new business from new customers. These new customers want to exploit the short lead time to fill in the gaps when their regular supplier fails or if they are trying to complete a large project and your part is the constraint. Do not give away this service for anything less than a significant premium. Remember, your competition cannot deliver in this timeframe or else these customers would not be coming to you. Experience has shown that you can offer the expedited service at no more than four times the normal price. Do not get greedy and offer your standard product at a higher price for standard guaranteed delivery. This will cause your customers to look elsewhere because they will feel exploited. For the new customers, you may want to offer your standard product at below market prices but with longer than market lead times. When the lead time is unacceptable, then the premium for the product will encounter less resistance because the lead time is also dramatically improved.

Conversely, when establishing the penalty you will offer to pay to the customer if you miss delivery, the penalty should be high enough to build the confidence of the client in the commitment to deliver the rapid service. In addition, the penalties should be high enough to block competition. Experience has shown that a penalty of 10% of the selling price per day of missed delivery is sufficient to pique the customer's interest and confidence that this is a valid offer.

Distribution

Distributors will grant business for proven excellent availability coupled with higher inventory turns at good prices. The limitation facing a distributor's ability to improve their profitability is that they suffer from both surplus and shortage simultaneously. Invariably they have too much of what they do not need and too little of what is actually selling. If your company sells through a distribution consolidation network then this solution may fit you. Typically the order lead time can be significant as the distributor attempts to consolidate orders to take advantage of quantity discounts or reducing inbound shipping costs. Since the distributor buys to a forecast and they deal with hundreds or thousands of part numbers, they tend to consolidate orders. Your customer may order from you once every two weeks. This is what leads to excess inventory since the quantities they are ordering tend to be large. Since cash is a critical constraint which causes the distributor to be very conservative in ordering and the part number is sold through many different points, the distributor will also tend to have shortages.

To sell this offer to your customer have them consider how many sales are lost to unavailability of a particular part or due to limited variety being offered to the retailer. This could also be inadequate display space being allocated by a retailer to a profitable product. Your offer could improve the customer's profitability by 30% or more because the space can be turned over quickly with higher profitability parts. A key measure for this is called GMROI—gross margin return on inventory. Think of having a dollar and you buy a part. You can sell that part for two dollars. You made a profit of one dollar. You have another part that you buy for a dollar and sell for $1.50. Clearly the first part is more profitable. But, consider that you can turn that second part over four times in the same time as it took you to sell the first part. That "less profitable" part has now made you $2.00 in profit in the same time the first part made only $1.00. GMROI can be expressed as a percentage of the inventory investment or as a multiple, in dollars, of your inventory invest-ment. That formula is GMROI (\$) = [gross margin (\$) ÷ aver-age inventory at cost].

This quickly becomes an unrefutable offer because if the product, quality, and prices are acceptable, you have reduced your customer's investment and risk. In return you enjoy more sales because of better availability, more products and better display of your products. You have stabilized the relationship because you now have a guaranteed reorder. This is a significant barrier for competitors. You also enjoy a smoother introduction of new products because you are now able to sense and respond to the changes in the product lifecycle. Last but not least, you will also enjoy slightly higher prices.

Similar to the quick response and VMI (vendor-managed inventory) solutions there is a penalty employed. The penalties build the customer's confidence in your ability to ensure avail-ability with much lower stock levels. These penalties also encourage your customer to promote your ability to deliver slow moving items or specials in fast delivery times. Most important-ly, the penalty offer differentiates your position from the compe-tition. Just like VMI, the trigger point for the penalty is the unavailability of the part and the penalty is paid each day the part is unavailable. In some cases, it is sufficient to offer penal-ties only if you are unable to replenish a stock-out within a day or two. For the slow moves or special items, the penalty is paid per day of missed delivery on the committed very short delivery time. This is very similar to the quick response approach.

To implement this process, the customer no longer places orders. They give you daily actual sales data. You then replen-ish these items immediately from the stock kept at your plant. For more detail on this approach, you can refer to *Necessary but not Sufficient.* Your production lead times must be consistently very short to ensure finished good availability at your plant with low levels of inventory otherwise the required high inventory level that would be necessary to do this fulfillment would cripple your company financially. In case of a large variety display, a restocking program is also implemented. The customer has the restocking option to replace items with other items. You make the recommendation on which items to hold based on your analysis of sales in the region. An approach for the large variety of very slow movers is to sell these items from a catalog or display rather than selling from stock—if the customer is willing to wait a short time.

On the pricing strategy, it is important that you do not increase your price until the approach is showing benefits. Waiting until the distributor actually sees the benefits makes the sell cycle much easier. Do remember when asking for the price increases that the distributor usually has very small margins so don't get greedy. In the case where there is a very high risk of a non-sale, offer a full refund rather than just an exchange. If at all possible do not get into the consignment model or VMI solution with the distributor.

Pay-for-Use

Large capital equipment is a difficult industry. The customer does not want to place an order for the equipment until they can prove that their demand is consistently higher than what they can produce currently. When they finally do order the equipment they want it delivered immediately. The equipment is highly engineered and customized to the end user's specification. The Pay-for-Use approach shifts the capital cost from the customer. You continue to own your machine and the customer pays you as it is being used. A press brake charges for each cycle. A photocopier charges for each copy. A tractor charges for each hour of use. Key to this approach is a counter of some sort that can record usage. The benefit to the customer is that they no longer have a large fixed asset. The machine is now a variable cost. As their production rises, the cost rises proportionately. The benefit to you is that the customer will order that machine far earlier and will pay more in the long run than if they had purchased it outright at the beginning. Similar to a car lease, there could be a residual value at the end if they desire to purchase it outright. In the agreement a baseline minimum use can be defined to ensure that the machine does not sit there idle.

As with the other offers, it is critical to create this value proposition as a win-win. Remember your desire is to sell more machines in a more linear fashion. To accomplish this you must make the offer unrefutable to the customer. Another value to wrap around the offer is to maintain the equipment as part of the bargain. The advantage for the customer is that they do not need to worry about the machine nor be liable for maintenance that was not done properly or done in a timely manner. The advantage to you is that if you need to move that piece of equipment elsewhere, you know it is well cared for.

Projects (bonuses – penalties)

The essence of the project offer is to guarantee the completion of a project not only on time and on budget but to earn a bonus for completing the project early. Conversely there is a significant penalty if you are late to your commitment. The customer would value this offer if time is a critical element and their desire is for completion as soon as possible. This is true when you are delivering part of a project that is feeding another project. If your part of the project is on the critical path for the main project then any time saved in your component saves time and potentially cost in the main project.

To be successful in this approach, a critical chain scheduling approach is necessary. If you do not currently manage projects with CCPM (critical chain project management), the next action is to embrace this methodology. See the short discussion of CCPM on page 126 in this chapter. The win-win is that you are able to earn significant bonuses for delivering projects early at no incremental cost to your operation.

Gain Sharing

Gain sharing suggests a collaborative relationship between you and your customer. This is used in some service industries as well as product industries. The underlying concept in gain sharing is that you are essentially selling your idea on improving the process and your customer's overall results. In an environment where there is a long contractual arrangement and customer maintains the design specification and the drawings, gain sharing can be as simple as an offer to share 50-50 any improvements made where drawings need to be updated by the customer. This sharing is done as a reduction in prices charged for the part. Other gain sharing can be done in a distribution or retail relationship where you provide information or specific product displays that improve overall profitability. This is further detailed in the throughput guarantee per shelf option on page 113.

To effectively enter into a gain sharing win-win relationship, there must be an ongoing relationship between you and your customer. Gain sharing requires an intimate knowledge of your customer's business and their constraint to increased profitability. A caution to implementation is that the performance measurement baseline and any actions required by your customer must be clearly defined. Getting that clarity in the face of such significant changes in the general industry can be quite difficult.

Availability Insurance

The essence of availability insurance is that you guarantee to have parts available immediately even in the face of spikes of demand. This works well with service parts with irregular demand or for buffer stocks of items that may have an external trigger to demand. An example of this could be air conditioners during the summer or fuel oil in the winter. Availability insurance requires you to hold a significant buffer that may never be used. Like the insurance industry, when several possible risks are pooled into one common area, the risk is spread across that pool. Also, like the insurance industry, the price may look high until it is needed and then the company will consider it money well spent. Establishing availability insurance requires an investment of company resources to hold the inventory and a sufficiently large market across which to spread the risk.

Throughput Guarantee Per Shelf

In the distribution solution the concept of GMROI was introduced. The throughput guarantee per shelf takes that concept to the next level. Fundamentally, you rent the shelf from the retailer for your product line. In return you guarantee the retailer a certain level of throughput from that shelf. You have the responsibility for the merchandising of that shelf meaning you select which products are included and how they are displayed. The retailer tracks sales through its point of sale system. At the end of each agreed upon period, you collaboratively examine the resulting throughput. Anything in excess of the throughput is paid back to you and any shortage is paid by you to the retailer. This process allows you to try new product combinations and determine what is selling or not selling and make quick adjustments. The retailer is responsible for sending daily consumption data so that you can replenish the sold items in a similar process to VMI as described on page 114.

Vendor Managed Inventory

The idea of vendor managed inventory is that you continue to own the inventory until the customer actually uses it. Customers will grant business for proven excellent availability coupled with lower inventory and less hassle at good prices. This solution is last on the list of strategic improvements because a VMI offer should be utilized only as a last resort. Once you offer VMI to a customer, you have few places from which to increase revenue. VMI should be offered only as a last resort and then only to the best customers. Based on actual consumption data rather than on orders from the customer, you manage the client's inventory and guarantee excellent availability with an overall reduction in inventory.

The VMI situation is similar to the quick response scenario on page 103. The customer is not completely satisfied with the balance between inventory and availability. For VMI to be considered as a possible solution, your customer must be placing repeat orders for the same part and they order this part relatively infrequently (once in 2-3 weeks). Also the value of this part cannot be negligible. When all these conditions are true then the customer is holding a not insignificant surplus inventory. The customer's willingness to wait is very small so the vendors are most likely producing to a forecast. Since forecasts are inherently wrong, then problems of availability are likely to exist. Factors that enhance the dissatisfaction include that the lifespan of inventory is relatively limited (not 100 times bigger than inventory) and there are occasional emergency orders (e.g. 3%).

For the VMI solution to work effectively, the production lead times defined in Chapter 5 must be consistently low. Technology is necessary to eliminate the order lead time by providing real-time visibility of end customer demand and inventory targets. Logistical constraints must allow very frequent deliveries to be done economically. When all these requirements are met, it is possible to deliver to the customer full availability of all parts with less than half the current inventory levels today. If these conditions are not met, your next step is operational improvement to develop this capability.

To sell this idea to your customer, you need to request all volume of the specific part number to come to your company. VMI is impossible with multiple companies providing the same parts. You gain exclusivity on selected parts. Once you have proven yourself on the initial group of parts then you can expand that exclusivity to other part numbers and product lines. This provides your company an increase in volume with that customer of course depending on your current share of that customer's business. Similar to quick response, this is an excellent way to service the gorilla in the supply chain when you are the canary. Depending on your previous relationship and pricing structure, you may be able to successfully negotiate a small premium (something on the order of 2-10%) for providing the additional service. Be careful about charging too much since you may push your customer to a competitor or to another solution. Probably more important than the premium is that this arrangement is usually a significant barrier for competitors since the ordering and replenishment is automatic. Other prospects for this offer are those prospects that generate high throughput for your company. The limit there is dictated by your capacity.

Remember that there is a guarantee associated with this offer. The penalty should not try to cover the damage to the client. The penalty should be high enough to build confidence in the customer that you are committed to ensure supply. From experience with this offer, the recommendation is a fixed price per day for each part that is not available. This fine should be large enough for the customer to know you care. When this process is first started at the customer, remember that a pilot approach works best. Begin with a higher buffer amount to raise the customer's confidence and as you gain experience and the customer gains confidence, you can reduce that amount. This offer can be set up as either a consignment model where the customer pays only for what is consumed when it is consumed. The customer will own significantly less inventory in either case. There needs to be an agreement in place on what happens to residual inventory in the event of an engineering change making the part in stock obsolete. The other more preferred approach is that the customer pays for the inventory on receipt. This still provides a significant reduction in inventory cost for the customer since you are shipping more frequently.

Be aware that this can be a very long sales cycle to convince the customer to put all their eggs in your basket. You will need to meet with different functional areas at the customer site. Remember that they will be skeptical of this offer until they see it working. The customer needs to understand that they will no longer be doing any of the activities related to purchasing, i.e., planning, orders, expediting, shuffling dates, quoting, batching, etc. They will be responsible for sending you the consumption data daily and you will replenish periodically according to your analysis and desired buffers. Once you have success at one client, you can then leverage the same approach to other appropriate clients. Remember that this offer is a last resort due to the lack of significant premium and that it absolutely spoils the customer leaving you no maneuvering room for other offers. Another downside is that this is very difficult to un-implement once deployed.

OPERATIONAL IMPROVEMENT SOLUTIONS

Lean

A major shift during the late 1980s and early 1990s was that the time to market was getting increasingly shorter. The first to market with a product made the most long-term profit. Lead times expected by the market continued to shorten and customers were no longer satisfied with the service level that was considered world class only a few years earlier. Customers were demanding to have their products delivered when, where and how they wanted them. Companies began to develop and embrace the philosophies of Just-in-Time (JIT) and supplier partnerships as a way to remain competitive. During the same period, the cost of goods sold was shifting drastically from labor to purchased materials. The Association for Manufacturing Excellence (AME) was formed to address the need for the development of new tools and techniques. APICS shifted from the "MRP Crusade" to the "Zero Inventory Crusade."

To bring some perspective to this shift, during the 1940s and 1950s it was not uncommon for a company to have 40-60% of the cost of goods sold contributed by labor costs. Given this fact, it was no wonder why companies automated and focused on the productivity of labor. Labor was the driving force for profitability. This was the major focus of the planning systems; get the material to the operation and never allow that operation to run out of work. It was better to have extra inventory than allow the operation to run out of work.

Beginning in the 1990s the focus shifted to material becoming the driving force for profitability. Many companies found that material had grown to 60-70% of their cost of goods sold while the labor cost declined to 10-20%. Major improvement in labor productivity only yielded small improvement in the overall company's profits. To improve the overall financial performance of the enterprise, the focus of the planning system logically shifted to effectively planning material and optimizing material utilization.

Investment in improvements in material utilization could result in big returns. Carrying extra inventory was no longer a competitive business practice.

At the same time, the response lead times expected by the market continued to shorten and customers were no longer satisfied with the service level that was considered world class only a few years earlier. Customers were demanding to have their products delivered when, where and how they wanted them. Companies began to develop and embrace the philosophies of Just-in-Time and supplier partnerships as a way to remain competitive. Competitiveness and profitability was now something that not only the production department focused upon, rather the whole enterprise had to be focused on this goal. All enterprise resources had to be aligned to those goals and integrated in their approach to reach the corporate objectives. No longer could departments launch things over the wall to the next department. Integrated resource management was the focus for a competitive company.

Just-in-Time received a great deal of recognition but the concept became increasingly entrenched in manufacturing enterprises under the term Lean Manufacturing. Lean Manufacturing is the next generation for Just-in-Time. Lean concepts include:

- ▸ **Identify product value stream:** Only those items which added value from a customer's perspective were identified

- ▸ **Flow:** Production should flow through the plant like water in a river—no pools of inventory or long waiting queues in front of machines.

- ▸ **Pull:** Production builds only what the customer wants when they want it. Since the lean concept provides the opportunity to build the same products in a fraction of the previous lead time, it is now possible to move from make-to-stock to a make to order strategy. This dramatically reduces obsolete inventory.

▶ **Eliminate waste:** Waste is defined as anything that does not add value to the product. This includes materials, manpower, capacity or any other resource.

▶ **Responsiveness to change:** Lean concepts are the method by which an enterprise becomes more agile to changes in the market.

▶ **Endless pursuit of perfection:** The cycle of improvement is never ending and continually focuses on the reduction of waste.

This text is not intended to be a complete discussion of Lean. For additional information please see the references at the end of this chapter. If this step is too big a leap for your organization, then see the organizational readiness section on page 129.

Six Sigma

The Six Sigma methodology was derived from the Total Quality Management arena led by Dr. Walter Shewhart and Dr. W. Edwards Deming. The Shewhart cycle of plan, do, check, act has been refined to Define, Measure, Analyze, Improve, Control. The Six Sigma approach will use the data inherent within a metric itself and analyze it (after understanding the process) through the use of tools such as Statistical Process Control, Numerical Evaluation of Metrics, or Design of Experiments. The breakdown and understanding of what drives the output metric will direct the development of solutions to achieve the target. The Six Sigma methodology is problem focused and strives to remove the variability from a process to generate a uniform process output. As a result there is less waste, faster throughput, less inventory, less fluctuation and improved overall quality.

This text is not intended to be a complete coverage of the DMAIC process for Six Sigma. If Six Sigma appears to be your next step, you may want to consider contacting the International Society of Six Sigma Professionals (www.isssp.com). If this step is too big a leap for your organization, then see the organizational readiness section on page 129.

DBR/BM (Drum Buffer Rope/Buffer Management)

Drum, buffer, rope and buffer management were introduced in *The Goal.* These concepts were further developed and expanded in context of the VAT plant types in Synchronous Management. The term "buffer" plays a very important role in the Theory of Constraints' (TOC) thinking. It has two critical uses:

a. As a critical part of any planning. Its role is to make the planning realistic in view of the variability in the environment. TOC strives to clearly define the "buffer" parts in the planning so the planner would be guided to think whether buffering is truly needed at that particular part of the planning and then also dedicate some thought as to how much buffer the plan truly needs.

b. In the execution stage, the actual use of the planned buffer is the kernel for the control method called Buffer Management. The idea is that as a buffer (protection mechanism) was clearly introduced into the planning, the actual consumption of the buffer is an indicator to the state of the plan as a whole. This insight brings huge benefits.

When the TOC manufacturing planning method, called Drum-Buffer-Rope (DBR), was developed (around 1984) the term 'buffer' was emphatically called 'time-buffer'. The argument is that in order to protect the on time shipping, or the schedule of the capacity-constraint-resource, what the planner can do is to release the appropriate materials so there is enough time for the parts to overcome Murphy. Certainly, the use of time-buffers is very appropriate for make-to-order environments.

Generally speaking the use of stock as a protection mechanism can be translated to time. It is customary to express stock in three different ways: Time, money and quantity. When a certain stock of parts is expressed as 'three weeks' we understand it as the average quantity that is predicted to be consumed in the next three weeks. On one hand it makes sense for us much more than "two hundred and forty six parts" when we try to assess whether the stock is too high or too low. On the other hand, would we be surprised if that stock would be consumed in four weeks or only in two weeks? So, expressing stock in time means using a forecast. Note, a forecast means deducing the future from the past. Describing the stock as "three weeks" is based probably on how fast this amount was consumed lately. The use of it for decision-making is the prediction "it'd be all gone in three weeks."

This inexplicit use of forecasting in expressing stocks is sometimes quite confusing. In determining the appropriate stock level the time element is very important. However, as we'll see TOC uses quantities and ratios of quantities for control purposes, and even for assessing whether the initial stock level determination needs updating. This is a relatively newer development of the use of stock buffers as integral part of both DBR and Buffer Management methods.

Stock buffers have to be used when the actual consumption of the stock cannot be predicted. In other words, when the tolerance time of the customer is shorter than the production lead-time. The reason for holding stock should be just that it is not possible to supply the final product on time unless we have stock of part X. Part X can be the finished product, or a common part component (in an assemble-to-order environment) or a raw material (even in a make-to-order environment). Protecting the market demand, coupled with too slow replenishment time, should be the sole cause for maintaining planned stocks.

Let's assume that in the vast majority of the cases management looks for very high service levels, without being too specific about it. In such a case the rule for determining the appropriate stock level should be that the "Maximum" forecasted consumption within the replenishment time factored by the level of unreliability of replenishment time. The term "maximum" is closely connected to the term "service level"—how much sales and operations management are prepared to fully support.

The term "unreliability of replenishment time" also targets to highlight the connection between service and possible lateness of the replenishment. What does the stock level mean? The above definition certainly points to the stock being a "buffer"—a protection mechanism. But do we really expect that at every point in time the buffer (the stock level) will be full? It is enough that some items would be sold today to reduce the actual buffer below the determined level. What can be done about that? The best that can be done is to replenish the items that were sold. But, those items, just pushed into the pipeline, need some time until they arrive to the buffer. This is exactly what the determination of the buffer/stock is supposed to do. It does not necessarily define how much stock is ready for immediate consumption; rather it defines how much stock should be both in the consumption point and in the pipeline.

As long as the replenishment level truly represents the "maximum" sales within the average replenishment time factored by the level of unreliability of the replenishment time, and as long as every sale initiates almost immediately an order to supply that quantity back—the service level would be very high and reliable.

Note that most of the current practices of maintaining stock put a lot of emphasis on forecasting the demand. But, the demand, even when it includes a good assessment of the variability (like the forecasting error), covers only one source of "noise." Most of those practices do not require the replenishment time, and not less important, the variability of the replenishment time.

The TOC logic is that improving the forecast should only pay insignificant dividends compared with any improvement in the replenishment time and reliability.

So, how does the above TOC practice succeed to lower the inventory in the system and, at the same time, improve the service level? The TOC rational is: make your best guess about the replenishment level, taking into account all four factors, and then monitor the actual consumption of the buffer. The replenishment level is considered to be a buffer. There is not much value is separating the average consumption from the variability. So, the quantity that ensures the appropriate service level is a buffer.

How should the user monitor the performance of the replenishment level? Here is where the three zones of the buffer are so helpful. The color of the zone denotes the priority. A buffer that is almost full is in the Green zone—no urgency whatsoever. When the actual end-item stock is in the Yellow zone—there is some urgency to bring in supply orders that are on their way. When the actual on-hand stock is in the "red," then the supply should be expedited.

The priorities in a true DBR/Buffer Management environment are set according to the "buffer status:" the percentage of the buffer consumed. For make-to-stock orders the buffer status is the percentage of the missing quantity to the replenishment level relative to the replenishment level. Suppose that the replenishment level is 120 units and right now 70 units are in stock and there are two orders in the way: one for 32 units and another one for 18. The status of the buffer is: 100*(120-70)/120=41.66%. That's a pretty good status—in the Yellow zone. Once the buffer status goes up to 66% then the buffer would penetrate into the red zone, and at least one of the orders would have to be expedited.

Monitoring the actual behavior of the stock buffer within the zones gives a clue whether the current replenishment level is about right or very wrong. If a penetration into the red zone is relatively common or the time the stock is below the red line is pretty long, then the replenishment buffer should be increased. The TOC recommendation is to enlarge it by a full zone. Once we do that it is recommended to wait for one replenishment time period until the buffer is checked again.

If the buffer was in the Green zone for a whole replenishment time without penetrating the Yellow zone even once—the buffer should be reduced. This way, monitoring the buffer creates simple and effective guidelines on how much inventory to hold, without any need for sophisticated forecast, that is by definition unreliable, and just looks at one half of the picture, only on the demand side, when the replenishment side is as important.

How should the TOC approach consider customer orders for certain future due-dates? The norm is to consider any firm customer order within the replenishment time horizon in order to issue the appropriate replenishment order. Thus, the replenishment level provides full protection just for the demand that cannot be predicted within the replenishment time period. It also protects the predicted demand from fluctuations that are too large in the replenishment. If this step is too big a leap for your organization, then see the organizational readiness section on page 129.

Critical Chain Project Management

The first rule of managing projects is quickly learned. After only a short time as a project manager, you discover all projects are completed late! To be competitive, projects must be completed on time. The reaction is to schedule more slack time for each event and be very conservative about the estimates of the activities on the critical path. This strategy lasts about as long as needed to get to the boss's or customer's office and then the project timeline is slashed putting the project manager back where they started—projects are always late. How can you find your way out of this viscous cycle? After a number of successful implementations over many years, Critical Chain Project management is the answer. The idea was taken from *Critical Chain*, written by Dr. Eli Goldratt, the first new development in project management in the last two centuries.

The root cause reason that projects are always late is the normal human response to multiple tasks is to prioritize by due dates. Even though the assigned tasks could be completed early other tasks always seem to come up and steal that capacity. How many times have you had a task to complete for weeks and you did not start it until the day before it was due? The same phenomenon occurs every day in projects balancing resources against multiple tasks. Provided the activity is completed by the late finish date—all is okay in the world of project management. Critical lead time is lost by using this strategy. How can a project be completed on time when all the slack time is consumed in the earliest stage of the project? The answer simply is that it can't. Expecting early finishes to balance out late finishes is only a figment of the scheduler's imagination. So how can you schedule a project to assure it will be completed on time without building in unacceptable slack time?

The reason for the schedule slack time is to guard against variability in the estimates given by the process owners. Classic project management teaches us to use optimistic, pessimistic and most likely estimates when scheduling a project. Quickly the project schedule becomes so complex to manage we just stick with the most likely estimate and the project is late more often than not. Complexity and variability once again rule the day. The safety lead time is just another way to guard against variability.

This variability can also be seen as output variability. Anyone that has managed a sequential manufacturing operation of any size knows that some days are very productive while others seem to have everything go wrong. The same phenomenon occurs in sequential project tasks. Overall output is less than expected. The most perfect product, when delivered late, is as useful as a bad product delivered on time. Either way the customer is not well served. The real culprit for the less than expected output is variability. Variability is found in every process in the plant, product, task or paperwork.

CCPM uses the optimistic estimate of the activity and gathers all the safety lead time and puts them at the end of the project. This unique focus puts real clarity on the true critical path and gathers all the recovery time into a clearly understood pool that can be better managed and utilized to assure project timeliness. Each activity is then held to its more aggressive dates and the queue is taken out between activities to reduce overall elapsed time and provide visibility of the real slack time. This takes excellent communication among everyone involved in the project to reap the benefits but the benefits are worth the cost and effort. Projects are completed on time and in significantly shorter lead time. How could your company turn that reality into a competitive advantage?

A very successful competitive strategy for a project driven company is lead-time. A company that can complete a quality project in less lead-time that the competition can typically demand a premium for this performance. Having inventory available at the earliest expected moment that the operation could begin can enhance lead-time response. This is not to say that all materials should be purchased at the beginning of the project. However, the better alternative to guessing when the activities with slack time will really start is to utilize Critical Chain scheduling. By using these resource schedule buffers, more accurate start dates are calculated with which to determine real material need. The more agile a company is in the execution of a project, the less opportunity there is for cost overruns due to unexpected crisis. Or in the immortal words of Marine Colonel William Scott (retired) in the management of a large aviation remanufacturing depot, "The longer the cow is in the pasture, the more grass it can eat!" A direct relationship exists between lead-time and cost. When the business processes are capable and agile, costs dramatically reduce. However, if the quick response time is accomplished by expediting and manual intervention, short lead-times can be financially disastrous. Anyone who has worked on a project that was behind schedule will attest to this fact. Schedule and cost can never be recovered simultaneously. Effective project management can provide a true competitive advantage. If this step is too big a leap for your organization, then see the organizational readiness section on page 129.

Organizational Readiness and Alignment

Possibly your organization is so dead set against change, or they have been around the block so many times they are just not willing to try another approach. If your team is not remotely interested in reading another book or has never taken a systematic approach seriously, then your first step is to get the excitement and interest in *Theory H.O.W., How Organizations Could Work* going. Start with simple company surveys asking for ideas to get people thinking and talking. Take the management team on a retreat to kick off the process. This approach requires a strong team atmosphere led by a person with a vision of the possible future. This is the time for you to step out and lead. You may be surprised who is ready to follow. Providing a clear direction (even if it is exactly the wrong direction) will create a sense of excitement and a buzz in the organization. Harness that energy and begin to move forward.

Do not be surprised if you discover that some organizational structure issues arise. Any company that has not taken a critical look at their structure and goals in a long time will find that it has evolved some degree of overlap and possibly distrust between departments. Introducing the Theory H.O.W. approach to your company is a great way to identify those overlaps. When these are eliminated, you will find that the overall morale of the organization improves and the team is now "open for business"—the improvement business that is. This organizational alignment will also enhance the success of any improvement project you choose as your next step.

Summary

In this chapter you used both the static and dynamic enterprise characteristics to identify a possible next step for your company. Depending on where your company is on the improvement continuum, the results of this project can be a strategic improvement step which will generate a significant contribution to your bottom line. Possibly you discovered that your company is not quite ready yet from an operational perspective to provide a reliable value proposition to the market. The operational improvement solution is your next step to prepare your company for that strategic improvement solution that can generate that big result. Maybe your company needs to start at the very beginning with organizational readiness and alignment. In any case, beginning with the end in mind provides wonderful context for your team. Everyone responds well to knowing where they are going and why. Whatever your next step is, *Theory H.O.W.* can provide an ongoing approach for your company.

References

Necessary but not Sufficient, Goldratt, Schragenheim, and Ptak
Critical Chain, Goldratt
The Goal, Goldratt
Synchronous Manufacturing, Srikanth
Quantum Leap: The Next Generation, Gilliam, Jones

Lean Manufacturing
    Lean Thinking, Womack, Jones
    Learning to See, Rother, Shook
    Implementing a Lean Management System, Jackson, Jones
    The New Lean Toolbox, Bicheno

Chapter 8
The Implementation Phase

Introduction

By this point, you have a deep understanding of the static and dynamic enterprise characteristics for your company. In addition, you have developed your vision, your goal, and selected your first strategic objective. In this chapter, you will develop an overall implementation plan for your first strategic objective and develop an understanding about the critical implementation issues you and your team will face.

Figure 8.1 **Developing the Implementation Plan**

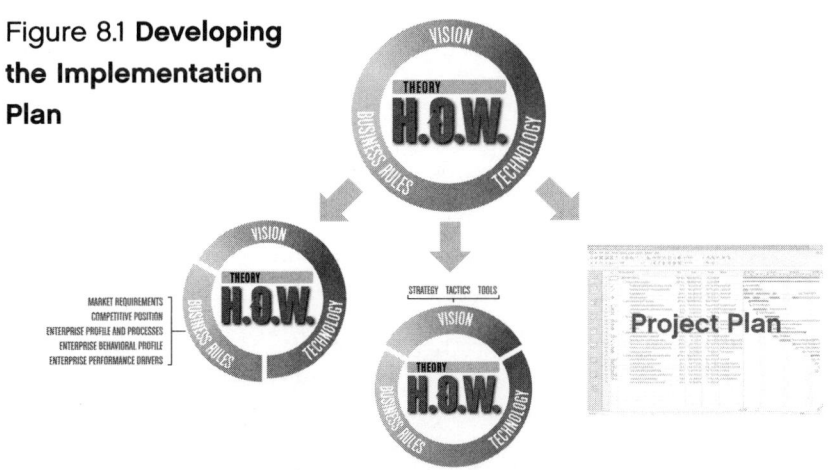

GET READY–PROJECT PLAN DEVELOPMENT

Introduction

The first step in any project should be to determine the objective or expected deliverable from the project. The Theory H.O.W. approach to this point has provided specific goals for your project. The important thing to remember is that whatever goal or objective is chosen; it should be meaningful to the enterprise as a whole. This provides the motivation for the project during the difficult times. The next step of the get ready phase is to determine the approach for the implementation. There are two basic possible approaches for implementation.

Do It Yourself Approach

The first approach is to accomplish the implementation entirely within the enterprise with no outside assistance. The benefit of this approach is that the out of pocket cost will be the lowest. However, if the expertise does not exist within the enterprise to accomplish the wide variety of tasks required in a project like this, the project could take much longer than expected and the returns could be very disappointing.

For this option to succeed, all involved personnel must be well acquainted with the underlying principles and techniques through an intensive educational effort.

To consider this implementation without having anyone inside the firm with significant previous implementation experience is a sure plan for disaster. Trying to go it alone without sufficient internal experience is being penny-wise and pound-foolish.

Hire Outside Resources

Another approach that many larger companies take is to contract for the additional resources required to accomplish the implementation. The different strategies for consultants were discussed in Chapter 3.

Scope Development

Whatever staffing approach is chosen, the overall implementation must include a clear statement of work describing the desired scope of the project. Scope creep is a very common phenomenon. Unfortunately, the budget was not developed with this increased scope and the costs can quickly spiral out of control without an adequate return on investment. The increased scope can mean that the project will never come to completion. This experience is very common and can be difficult to control if there is insufficient scope control at the beginning of the project. The form below illustrates an excellent format to begin the process of a detailed project plan. This begins to align your activities from the strategic to the tactical. The high level tasks

Figure 8.2 **Strategic Initiative: Tactical Plan Development Form**
Breakthrough Program / Improvement Project Name

What is the Dynamic Enterprise Characteristic (DEC)	Describe the Current Key Problems / Challenges	Describe the Key Opportunities		
Describe Initiative Key Objective (s)	Time Frame for Project	List Project Success Criteria and Measures		
Project Champion / Sponsor	Team Members	Project Assumptions		

Tactical Plan – Tasks	Action Plans	Who	When	Comments

outlined using the form can be further defined, expanded, and managed through the use of any Project Management Tool.

Project Resources

When managing an implementation, there are three control knobs; scope, resources, and time. If the scope of the project is reduced, the project should take less time. If the resources are reduced, the time required will be longer. Finding the resources to support the implementation can be the most difficult issue to face. Two successful approaches can be taken. One is to bring in temporary help for the routine duties. These temporaries can be low wage people to perform the repetitive tasks. The concern is that supervising the temporaries might take more time than the extra save. Another type of temporary is a college intern. These interns are usually well educated but do not have practical experience. They can be used to augment the team during the implementation and are usually very quick in coming up to speed in the organization. This opportunity provides them work experience and the company the extra resources needed at a reasonable price—a winning combination for both parties involved.

The second way to free resources is to begin doing the existing job differently. Each task that is currently being done must be examined to see if it really adds value to the organization or just adds work. Many people are very busy working hard, but are accomplishing little. Many daily tasks are done without their need being challenged because "we have always done things that way." The most important part of the implementation process is the re-engineering of current process. There is no time like the present to begin the process! Examining the processes for value can dramatically reduce modification requested from the system.

Part of the reengineering process requires many decisions to be made. The decision process is just one of many processes that must be established early in the project. The implementation team should be from a sufficient level in the organization to be able to make decisions that the organization will implement. The implementation team should expect to experience the normal team evolutionary steps of forming, storming, norming and performing. These steps mean that the implementation team must first be selected from the appropriate level of the organization. Given the high quality level of personnel involved in the project, conflict is normal and should be expected. Having a well-defined process for incorporating innovation and conflict resolution into the implementation will provide the best results.

Budget

The exact budget is determined in detail by the specific approach taken by the company. Don't forget to include how much outside assistance is needed for the implementation. Part of the budgeting process is an expected timeline for the investment and the anticipated return. The budget must include the resource models and the overall assumptions made for the project. This should be well-documented early in the process so that later in the project these assumptions can be easily identified.

GET SET

Introduction

The get set phase also includes identifying the roles and leadership required for the successful implementation. Leaders are found in many areas of the enterprise. Many times the real leaders are not those with the senior title but rather those that demonstrate the traits of leadership. These informal leaders must be carefully aligned with the overall system implementation goals. One way to obtain that commitment is through education. Education provides the overall understanding of what the company is attempting to implement and why. The first step on the road to competitiveness is a common understanding of the destination. Every journey is easier when the final destination is well understood and communicated.

Education

Rarely does a small company have the resources for a full-time internal trainer. This means that this crucial education must be secured from outside the organization. The need for education cannot be stressed too strongly. Imagine entrusting an accountant with no education the responsibility of preparing financial statements. No sane business owner would make that move. As a sage advisor once said: "If you think education is expensive, try ignorance." Education is required for all employees to actively participate in a successful implementation. Well meaning people can do exactly the wrong thing for the right reasons.

Roles and Responsibilities

Two other areas that must be considered in the get set phase are the roles and responsibilities for different functional areas in the project. Refer back to the Preparation Phase in Chapters 3 & 4.

Select Project Team

This team should have a common vision of the implementation's goal. The best people selected for this team are not the people who can afford to be away from their regular job to support the implementation. The project team is made of those people who are the core of the business. Relieving some of their regular workload is needed to provide the time the implementation will require. It is not possible for these people to continue to perform their entire regular job in addition to the implementation. Skimping on the competency of the project team reflects directly in the implementation results. Don't you really want your best people working on your future?

Change Management–Effective Communications

A great deal of change can be expected during any implementation. To successfully manage change, communication is essential in assuring a constructive and positive climate and atmosphere surrounding the implementation. When problems are encountered, they should be communicated early to the affected personnel. If the team attempts to hide problems and issues there will develop an overall mistrust of the entire implementation. In the void of real facts and information, the affected personnel will fill in with their own ideas and rarely do these ideas reflect reality. One way to assure the appropriate climate is to confidentially survey the affected personnel by asking how the change is perceived; if the area is ready and how well the change is supported. When this index is tracked over time, problem areas can be more readily identified and resolved through improved communication or education. If these trouble spots are ignored, then larger problems will surely surface later in the implementation.

Many companies use an implementation newsletter to keep all areas apprised of the pending changes or challenges. Another frequently used communication process is the company bulletin board, intranet Website or company meetings. No matter how it is accomplished, effective communication is essential to ensure the best possible climate and atmosphere for the implementation.

Effective Project Communication

As your company begins the process of implementation, the organization will need to be constantly updated on the progress. As described in the Learning Phase, a project structure must be developed. The Executive Committee needs to provide the Implementation Team with direction and quick conflict resolution. The Implementation Team needs to report to the Executive Committee on the overall progress, results and issues. The Program Manager needs to communicate to the Implementation Team on the day to day activities. Your company and your consulting partner (if you choose to use one) need to have frequent communication to keep the project on target. The entire organization as a whole needs to be constantly reminded as to the goals and direction of the project in order to remain focused on the goal.

An excellent way to manage the project and communicate across the company is through a "project room." Meetings can be held in this room and critical measures reviewed holistically about the project. The intent of the project room is to foster open communication across functional groups and assist in building a teamwork atmosphere for solving problems and resolving important issues. This approach supports the continuous improvement efforts and improves accountability for corrective actions. The project room should incorporate a complete set of dynamic enterprise characteristics as well as key performance indicators.

Figure 8.3 **The Operations Project Room Meeting**

Sample Wall Layout: Create an 'end-to-end' view of the process and how we are doing

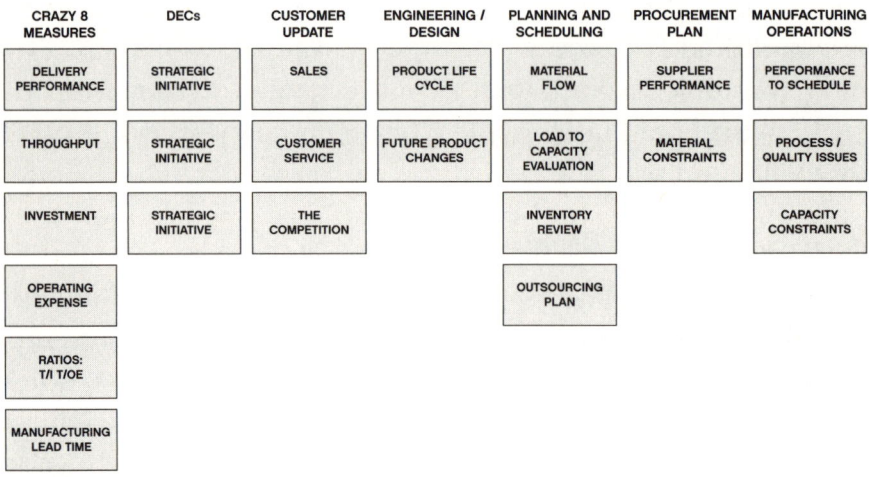

The status room meeting should have representation from each of the key area in the organization (sales, manufacturing, procurement, engineering, customer service, quality, information systems)

The role of the facilitator is to prepare and run the meeting based on a script developed by the team. The purpose of the script is to foster consistency as well as to document the process so others can step in as required. The script will change as the team gets more comfortable with the process and you get better at communicating.

The team is responsible for making sure that the charts and measures that are required from their areas are updated in the room prior to the meeting. They are also responsible for reporting on the status of their performance during the meeting.

Document Policies and Procedures

This last task is the one that frequently does not get done effectively. Documenting policies and procedures is not glamorous work. Documenting policies and procedures is an excellent place to use a college intern. Policies and procedures do not have to be the thickness of War and Peace to be effective. The best policies and procedures are no more than one page, front and back. The policy statement of what is intended to be accomplished is on the front. The procedural steps to accomplish that objective are detailed in a flowchart format on the back. What could be simpler? This approach is consistent with ISO 9000 and will not bury the plant in paperwork. A better solution is to have the procedure online and accessible at a click. Even online, remember that quality is not measured by the pound but rather by how well these procedures are utilized on a daily basis. Experience has shown that these one-page procedures often get posted on the wall or file cabinet for quick reference by their users. Isn't that how polices and procedures should be used, rather than collecting them in a book to gather dust on a shelf?

Measures & Metrics

In Chapter 6 you defined your company's critical dynamic enterprise characteristics. In Chapter 7 you selected the best project based on where your company is currently at given those dynamic enterprise characteristics. Defining a clear project scope includes the expected impact to those critical measures.

GO!

Introduction

Once all the planning and preparation has been completed, it is time to really begin the implementation process. Beware analysis paralysis. It is all too easy to never really feel sufficiently ready to move forward. On the flip side, remember what it feels like in a big crunch time when everything is clicking and things are just rocking? You are in the zone! This is the level of productivity and energy that is possible on a routine ongoing basis without the crisis. Just imagine what would be possible in your organization if the entire team was in the zone routinely!

Launching your Project & Change Management

Remember that this is a big change for your company. You need to consider how you are going to introduce the whole idea of this change to the organization. How are you going to "kick off" the project? This is a critical phase since it sends a message to the whole organization and for the entire duration of the project. Every organization is slightly different in personality but there are some basic rules that apply to every organization.

Remember to tune into "WIIFM" or "What's in it for me?" This project will impact everyone in the organization and they need a clear understanding of how they can make a contribution not only to the project but also how the project impacts the overall company in a significantly positive manner. There will be several different issues to address surrounding people:

▸ Attitude that can be either positive or negative.

▸ Personal capability that can be weak, capable, stretched, or strong.

▸ Two major behavior groups, either watchers and followers or drivers and leaders.

▸ Personalities such as introverts and extroverts.

▸ Dedication to the projects as either saboteurs or heroes.

Remember that the right people, in the right place, with the right tools and the right attitude can work miracles.

You may encounter resistance to this change. Debra Smith in her book *Measurement Nightmare* describes six layers of resistance to change. The reasons for resistance to change can be boiled down to six layers. For each layer of resistance to change, there are also six stages of buy-in. These layers must be handled in a sequential manner. For any significant change, to skip any one of the layers of resistance or stages of buy-in would be like building a house on only part of a foundation. The short term benefit will be more than overcome by the long term negative impact. Significant time will be lost as the organization must go back to those items not covered in the change process.

Figure 8.4 **Six Layers of Resistance**	Six Stages of Buy-In
1. Disagree on the problem	1. Agreement on the problem
2. Disagree on the direction of the solutions	2. Agreement on the direction of the solution
3. Disagree that the solution solves the problem	3. Agreement that the solution will yield the desired results
4. Claiming that the solution will also lead to negative effects	4. Agreement that no disastrous side effects will result
5. Pointing to obstacles blocking the implementation of the solutions	5. Agreement on the implementation requirements and the plan itself
6. Unverbalized fear	6. Agreement by all key collaborators that they can move forward with confidence

© *The Measurement Nightmare*, Debra Smith

1. **Agreeing on the problem**—this is a critical first step in the change process. Many great ideas exist in every organization. However, these solution ideas each solve different problems. People become quite enamored with their own idea and will defend it vigorously. Understanding the real problem includes the reasons this is a problem. What are

the undesired effects of this problem? How do these undesired effects impact each other? How long has this been a problem? Why have we put up with it for so long? What is the feasibility of solving the problem? We all may want to solve world poverty but alone this is not a feasible problem to solve. A problem is truly well understood if an identified major reason is eliminated and the effect it was causing is also significantly reduced. This critical analysis gives excellent insights into the real cause of the problem. This analysis can provide a very different answer than what was expected. Many times just this part of the process will solve the problem since there is now a clear description of the causes and effect.

2. **Agreeing on the direction of the solution**—This discussion should surface the assumptions behind the requirements for the suggested solution. Inherently there usually is some form of standing conflict that is causing the problem. The organization has attempted to compromise between the two divergent points of that conflict. The organization is finding that compromise is not working. Instead, the organization spends time on one side of the conflict until the undesirable effects from the strategy can no longer be tolerated. Then the organization flips over to the other side of the conflict. The organization continues with that strategy until the undesirable effect from that side of the conflict can no longer be tolerated. This process is repeated over and over, frustrating everyone in the organization. Understanding the real cause behind that conflict and the assumption under that conflict provides excellent insight on the direction of the solution. When raising the assumptions behind the conflict, breakthrough thinking is possible. This solution may be very different than expected. The assumptions that were thought to be fixed in concrete sometimes are more easily changed than expected.

3. **Agreeing that the solution will yield the desired results—** This step in the change process provides clear effect-cause-effect logic on how the suggested solution will move the organization from its current state to the desired future state. Insights gained from the previous two steps provide the roadmap for this step. In this step it is very important that the steps in the effect-cause-effect logic are not too big. Everyone involved in the project must understand how the future state will be achieved.

4. **Agreeing that the solution will not result in any disastrous side effect—**This is where the naysayer—the "yes—but" people have a place to shine. Change is always an emotional issue. Sometimes this emotion is positive and sometimes negative. Providing the opportunity for even the most negative person to review the plan, make their comments including all the things they know won't work and then have those ideas incorporated into the plan brings even the most difficult on board to the change. By addressing these reservations in the implementation plan, not only do these people feel like they have been heard but the overall project is more likely to succeed since the potential disasters have been identified and prevented.

5. **Agreeing on the implementation requirements and the plan itself—**This step further defines the things that block us from getting there. These can be physical things, policies, or informational issues. Similar to the previous step, this phase brings the naysayer from the sidelines directly into the process. Not only is their knowledge leveraged in the change, their concerns are directly addressed.

6. **Agreement by all key collaborators that they can move forward with confidence—**Large changes in a company bring people to the unknown. People fear the unknown. Many

times it is difficult to express that fear and what is causing it. With the robust process that was just described in the previous five steps there is now clear understanding of the problem, the direction of the solution and how the solution solves the problem. In addition, the obstacles and negative possible consequences have been addressed and a mitigation plan put in place. If there has been good participation by the team, then there should be a strong sense of confidence about the success for the project.

Failure Strategies

When attempting an implementation of this scope the following items can cause significant problems:

1. **Lack of education**—This does not mean a lack of degrees and diplomas. People with PhDs and MBAs are well-educated people but these degrees do not include in depth understanding of process improvement. If these subjects are covered at all, it is typically part of a single semester treatment of the subject.

2. **Lack of top management vision and active participation**—This lack of active participation will ensure failure of the implementation. Top management must provide the resources and motivation when the difficult times arise in the implementation. Without a clear understanding of the status and details of the implementation this support will not be possible.

3. **Allowing the consultants to do it for you**—If you are too busy to do the implementation with your own resources, hiring outside people to do it will ensure that the implementation will most likely look like the last implementation they did rather than fitting the specific needs of your business. Abdicating the responsibility of the company's future to outsiders will be met with resistance by the people who

have to change processes and procedures without a clear understanding of how it fits their needs. Change management is more difficult and the probability for success is close to zero. Consultants can provide excellent insights and a variety of experiences to the implementation. They have a place in a successful implementation; however consultants should be a resource to the implementation and not take over the implementation.

4. **Analysis paralysis**—The fear of making a mistake can paralyze the implementation team. The team waits for direct instruction from senior management that will never come. Senior management should not be involved at this level of detail. This is why the implementation team exists. Unempowered implementation teams will fear making a mistake and will continue to analyze a situation and delay action. This paralysis can stop an implementation in its tracks. Defining every problem or challenge before implementation is impossible. Cross-functional teams identify the likely potential problems and issues that can be identified. However, other problems may arise and this should not be punished. A team that does not fear retaliation is more capable of solving the problems that will arise.

5. **Being penny-wise and pound-foolish**—This is potentially a large investment for any company. Saving cost where possible is one way to improve the return on investment. However, the company needs to spend adequate money to ensure that sufficient quality is purchased in hardware, software, education and consulting services. Making a purchase based solely on cost can result in getting exactly what you paid for.

6. **Not challenging the status quo**—The implementation must begin to ask questions about the current processes and what

adds value or only cost. A company that is not continuously improving will be quickly overtaken by the competition.

7. **Cowboy implementation approach**—Shoot first, ask questions later. In the cowboy implementation approach little planning is done and the implementation moves off at breakneck speed. Quickly, routine problems that could have been prevented arise and can take the implementation off track into failure. In the hurry to get things done, nothing gets done because there has been no planning. An implementation team never plans to fail, but frequently fails to plan.

8. **Lack of communication to the affected users**—Having an implementation team work away from the main department isolates the users from the changes that will be needed to make the implementation successful. A key success strategy is communication, communication, and communication. Failure to communicate will cause the rumor mill to fill in the blanks and rarely is this 'fill' constructive or accurate.

9. **Trying to go it alone**—In the attempt to save cost, one strategy is to attempt the implementation without any outside help. Some outside expertise and guidance is required in almost every implementation. Having a knowledgeable outsider on the steering committee to oversee progress and ask the right questions can save far more expense that it costs.

Celebrate Success

This can be the most important step. The journey has been worthwhile. The whole company has just completed a major project. Celebrating recognizes this accomplishment and clearly demonstrates the importance to the company. This step is frequently forgotten. The celebration can be as simple or complex as you can imagine. Rewards can be free soda or coffee machines for a period of time. A favorite is a cookout where the management team cooks and serves the meal. Other ideas can be a picnic on company time with the rest of day off or a long weekend. If you began the process with a retreat, this is also a great idea to close out the project. Do not overlook this critical step. Remember that this is a continuing process so once the celebration is over it is time to start again.

Summary

Selecting a strategic objective and successfully implementing it fully in the company can appear overwhelming. Using a few simple tools, success in the form of significant bottom line results can be achieved in very short time. The most important tool in the implementation toolbox is education. Attempting to implement what is not well understood is always difficult and almost always impossible. A common vision of the goal and clear expectations of the outcome including benefits to the company expedites the whole process. Avoiding the known pitfalls and following the proven success strategies can result in bottomline benefits for your company—now and into the future.

Chapter 9
Summary

Competitive forces today are at a level never before seen in business. What worked before no longer works today. Doing what was done before and expecting similar results is not possible due to the impact of technology and other competitive forces. What is competitive today will just not be competitive in the future. You need to be always ready to answer three deceptively simple questions:

▶ Where will we be allowed to make a profit?

▶ What is our value proposition?

▶ What will drive profit and shareholder value?

Figure 9.1 **Theory H.O.W. Approach Summary**

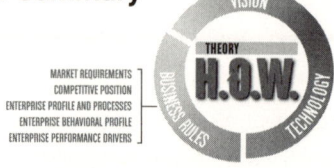

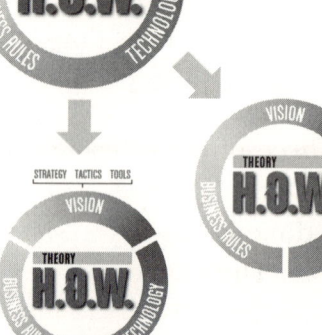

A different approach is necessary to ensure your success now and into the future. Together we have ventured on that approach in *Theory H.O.W., How Organizations Could Work*. We began with the evolution of management through Theory X, Theory Y, Theory Z and now *Theory H.O.W.* The Theory H.O.W. approach brings focus to what will generate the highest level of financial return for your company. Beginning with the Preparation Phase and continuing in the Learning Phase you prepared for you and your company to embark on this journey. In the Diagnostic and Improvement phases you developed your vision and picked your first project. The implementation phase brought that first project to reality. After achieving your first strategic objective, do not sit on your laurels. Do not allow inertia to settle in. There is still much to be done. The next phase is to go back to Chapter 5 and review the static enterprise characteristics quickly before delving right back into the diagnostic phase in Chapter 6. This will allow you to sustain this momentum.

Remember the fundamental ground rules.

▶ Every organization has a goal.

▶ The global organization is more than the sum of its parts.

▶ The performance of an organization is limited by very few critical variables.

▶ Even the most complex organization is subject to cause and effect relationships.

The three dimensions of success are vision, business rules, and technology. Like fire, and the need for oxygen and fuel, if one of these dimensions is removed then breakthrough results are not possible. The concept of Archimedes on Fire brings the focus to the constraint of your company that prevents you from achieving your goal.

To go from your vision to selecting the right business rules in a process of ongoing improvement:

- ▸ Identify the system constraint.

- ▸ Decide how to exploit the system constraint(s).

- ▸ Subordinate everything to the above decision.

- ▸ Elevate the system constraint.

- ▸ Go Back to step 1. Beware of inertia.

Technology is necessary, but not sufficient for the improvement process. Technology can provide an improvement, if and only if, it addresses the constraint in your company. The rules to success-fully exploit the technology are to be able to answer the follow-ing questions:

- ▸ What is the main power of the technology?

- ▸ What limitation does it diminish?

- ▸ What rules helped us to accommodate the limitation?

- ▸ What rules should we use now?

- ▸ In light of the change in rules, what changes are required in the technology?

- ▸ How to cause the change?

Soon this process of ongoing substantial improvement will become second nature. You will see people naturally using the Theory H.O.W. tools and techniques in their everyday business process. No longer will it be as strange as signing your name with your non-preferred hand.

Theory H.O.W. is about dramatically changing your results by changing how you and your people think.

Remember that "one thing" that is your competitive position in the market. What is it that is unique about your company that provides value to your customers at a profit to yourself? This is the banner that must remain in front of the team as they move towards the future. Soon you will see your team operating in that almost magical zone of improved productivity and creativity. Remember to reward that behavior and encourage the team through its successes and failures.

We have enjoyed being your guide during this journey. We welcome your feedback, thoughts, and experiences.

Harold E. Cavallaro
Carol A. Ptak

References

Theory Z, William Ouchi

Lean Thinking : Banish Waste and Create Wealth in Your Corporation, Revised and Updated by Womack, et. al.

The Goal, Goldratt

TOC and its Implications on Management Cost Accounting, Smith, et. al.

Introduction to Type, Briggs Myers

Attitude Is Everything, Meyers

Synchronous Management, Umble, Srikanth

Necessary but not Sufficient, Goldratt, Schragenheim, and Ptak,

Critical Chain, Goldratt

Synchronous Manufacturing, Srikanth

Quantum Leap: The Next Generation, Gilliam, Jones

Lean Thinking, Womack, Jones

Learning to See, Rother, Shook

Implementing a Lean Management System, Jackson, Jones

The New Lean Toolbox, Bicheno

Recommended Reading

Theory of Constraints

- *The Goal: A Process of Ongoing Improvement,* Goldratt, Cox; North River Press Publishing Corporation; ISBN: 0884270610; 2nd revised edition; [1992]

- *Theory Of Constraints,* Goldratt, Cox; North River Press Publishing Corporation; ISBN: 884270858; 2nd Revised edition; [1990]

- *Necessary but not Sufficient: A Theory of Constraints Business Novel,* Goldratt, Schragenheim, Ptak; North River Press; ISBN: 0884271706; [2000]

- *Regaining Competitiveness: Putting The Goal To Work,* Srikanth, Cavallaro; Spectrum Management Group; ISBN: 0943953006; [1987]

- *Synchronous Management: Principles For World-Class Excellence,* Umble, Srikanth; Spectrum Management Group; ISBN: 0943953073; [1990]

- *The Haystack Syndrome: Sifting Information Out Of The Data Ocean,* Goldratt; North River Press Publishing Corporation; ISBN: 0884270890; 2nd Revised edition; [1990]

- *Throughput Accounting,* Corbett; North River Press Publishing Corporation; ISBN: 0884271587; [1998]

Lean Manufacturing

▶ *Lean Thinking*, Womack, Jones; Simon & Schuster; ISBN: 0684810352; 1st edition; [1996]

▶ *Learning to See*, Rother, Shook, Womack, Jones; Lean Enterprise Institute; ISBN: 0966784308; [2003]

▶ *Implementing a Lean Management System*, Jackson, Jones (Contributor); Productivity Press; ISBN: 1563270854; [1996]

▶ *The Lean Toolbox*, Bicheno; PICSIE Books; ISBN: 0951382993; 2nd Edition; [1999]

▶ *Lean Transformation: How to Change Your Business into a Lean Enterprise*, Henderson, Larco, Martin (Editor); Oaklea Pr; ISBN: 0964660121; [1999]

▶ *The New Manufacturing Challenge: Techniques For Continuous Improvement*, Kiyoshi Susaki, Free Press; ISBN: 0029320402; [1987]

▶ *The Visual Factory: Building Participation Through Shared Information*, Greif; Productivity Press; ISBN: 0915299674; [1991]

▶ *The Quantum Leap: The Next Generation*, Gilliam, Jones, Ptak; J.Ross Publishing; ISBN: 1932159444; [2005]

Performance Measures

▶ *Measurement Nightmare: How the Theory of Constraints Can Resolve Conflicting Strategies, Policies, and Measures*, Smith; CRC; ISBN: 1574442465; [1999]

▶ *Measurements for Effective Decision Making: A Guide for Manufacturing Companies*, Srikanth, Robertson; Spectrum Publishing Company; ISBN: 0943953049; [1995]

Six Sigma

▶ *Six Sigma for Managers*, Brue; McGraw-Hill; ISBN: 0071387552; [2005]

Getting Things Done

▶ *Execution: The Discipline of Getting Things Done*, Bossidy, Charan, Burck; Crown Business; ISBN: 0739302752; [2002]

Systems

▶ *MRP and Beyond: A Toolbox for Integrating People and Systems*, Ptak; Irwin Professional Publishing; ISBN: 0786305541; [1996]

▶ *ERP, Tools, Techniques and Applications for Itegrating the Supply Chain*, Ptak, Schragenheim; CRC; ISBN: 1574443585 [2003]

List of Figures

List of Figures

Index

Index

Index

Accompanying
Tool